Umbrellas of Edinburgh

Poetry and Prose Inspired
by Scotland's Capital City

Umbrellas of Edinburgh

Poetry and Prose Inspired
by Scotland's Capital City

Edited by
Russell Jones and Claire Askew

Cover and illustrations by
Nick Askew

This edition published 2020
First published 2016

Shoreline of Infinity
8 Craiglockhart Bank
Edinburgh, EH14 1JH
www.shorelineofinfinity.com

ISBN 978-1-8381268-2-7

Typeset in Plantin

the publisher acknowledges investment from
Creative Scotland toward the publication of this book

Contents

East

Preface

In this book eighty writers respond to the challenge: 'choose a location in Edinburgh and write about it.' Straight and simple. Yet as you're about to witness, this has given rise to a myriad trove of variegated perspectives, voices and worlds. Edinburgh, here, becomes the multifarious sum of diversely enchanted, slanted, elated, deflated, rich, weird, splendid, cacophonous and sonorous works.

Writing about a place might seem a very basic thing for writers to do. But pick it apart a little. The place is always coloured by the perceiver, and the perceiver is always coloured by the place. The poem is an artful conjunction of two highly complex entities. More than this, the place will always be a space in time, so that no place can be the same place twice, just as no person remains static. And this is before we begin to think of what a poem is, or might be. A poem implies living language and shape or pattern. But what are these? They are not monolithic or simple entities, that's for sure.

If eighty writers were to choose a location in any single town or city in the world, and write about it, one might expect multiplicity. But there's something captivating about Edinburgh. All great cities have their own literary traditions, their own seed-bed of codes. But start writing about Edinburgh and it's hard not to feel that every stone in the place is a stereotype, every vista an archetype. It was no help to these writers that Edinburgh is a UNESCO World heritage site, with over 4500 listed buildings, as well as the world's first UNESCO City of Literature. Such an apex of heritage, for the writer seeking to speak to today, might as well be a vortex. And yet the depth and pull of the city's codes intoxicate the imagination. The in-your-face actuality of its symbolic allure, seeping from its streets as you go about your day, and night, cannot be ignored.

Named in the 10th century Pictish Chronicle as 'oppidum

Eden' (gaining its burgh in the early 12th century) and contained within its own walls for at least the following 500 years, Edinburgh grew upwards, stacked high with multi-storey buildings, where the social low and high occupied differing floors of the same tenements. Noted in the early C18th as one of the most thronged and putrid cities in Europe, the bourgeoisie would eventually, of course, move across to the 'New Town', whence one of the most archetypal urban psycho-geographies of the Western world would develop. To this day it is difficult to conceive of Edinburgh outside of oppositions: the old and the new; the light and the dark; the teeming and the spacious; the fine and the feral. Yet in the most compelling experiences of the contemporary city, these aren't segregated but are simultaneous.

Perhaps fundamental to the imaginative lure of Edinburgh is its trick of being at once circumscribed yet seemingly bottomless. The place is physically hemmed in by its hills and the firth, it's not huge. To the eye, when you're up in those hills, it's all there, in its entirety. But try and catch what is there. As a single yet shifting entity, then, Edinburgh provides an obvious immediacy of solidity and flux, permanence and variegation in terms of geography, history and architecture. Indeed, the place might also be defined through the ever-changing quality of its light, where the self-same vista can be entirely transmogrified in atmosphere and character in the space of minutes, sometimes seconds. But especially to the writer, the life of the place is even more intensely channeled through its language. Shaped by its hills, I've often wondered if the place looks, from above, like a mouth. Certainly, it lives, noisily, through many mouths.

Entrenched and widening material inequality is an obvious reality in Edinburgh, as in most places. But in at least some parts of the city, the way in which differing classes overlap makes this a pervasive reality, rather than something entirely photo-shopped out of the coffee-shop existence of its civic life. It has its ghettoes, of course, dispiritingly marginalized to the edge of town, as well as its protected fine spots for the fabulous few.

But in certain parts of the city differing classes still stack the same streets together. And this is something one hears, first and foremost, leading to a particularly vibrant oral life. The middle class and the poorer class each have distinct way of talking in Edinburgh, and both are wonderful. Add to this the verbal diversity brought by its many welcome visitors (a fifth of the city's population, at any one time, are students) and immigrants, and you are left with a brilliant Babel. To sit on a bus and listen to the chatter, in Edinburgh, is a wonder for the health of any prospective poet. The many-tongued murmuration of the city is a deep song for the ear.

On top of this, there is the matter of style. Edinburgh has its own backstory of competing literary styles, the usual penumbra of 'experimental' versus 'traditional', and so on. The contributors to this book hail from widely differing stylistic corners of the city of literature, as well as from differing physical places. And the resulting eclecticism found within these covers most truly reflects the life of writing, in this city and in Scotland more generally. A cornucopia of style just about sums the place up. Whether indigenous or international, it doesn't matter: the seventy writers in this book have listened, looked, felt deeply and applied their craft. Whether passing through, or here for generations, each writer has added to the poetry of the place. What follows is a perfect new volume for a contemporary Edinburgh – one book, many worlds; an abundance of places within one space.

Alan Gillis

Introduction

Scotland's capital is a vibrant, diverse and modern city, cultivated by people from around the world. It's filled with cutting edge art, international cuisines, theatres and pubs, bright minds and masonry, dark side streets and sinister stories. Edinburgh is a hub for literary inspiration and ambition, hosting the world's largest literary festival, and it's the world's first UNESCO City of Literature. But pick up a collection of writing about Edinburgh, and you're often faced with the same list of names: dead white men.

Robert Burns, Walter Scott and Hugh MacDiarmid (et al) deserve their place in anthologies and history books, but modern Edinburgh has so much more to offer its contemporary readers. Edinburgh evolves, and those changes are embodied in the city's literature. Our hope for this book as editors, then, is to provide new ways of looking at Scotland's capital, to offer a mouthpiece for its assorted voices.

Why an anthology of writing? Well, we believe that anthologies are important: they capture a sense of place and the concerns of their time, bringing together perspectives and voices to better express things that might otherwise be ignored. The kaleidoscopic views present in anthologies act to build a more intricate and prismatic picture than that which we might see from a single author.

As editors, we were keen to reflect the diversity of Edinburgh and its people, and to shift the existing (dead white men) focus through a more contemporary lens. This anthology includes work from writers of colour, writers who identify as LGBTQIA+, writers who live with disabilities, writers who have lived in countries other than Scotland, and its contributors predominantly identify as women.

Our brief to the writers was simple: choose a location in Edinburgh (from a very long list!) and write about it. Between these pages you'll find explorations of architecture, fragments of memories, views of potential futures, romps in hedgerows, summer picnics, hard winters, love, loss and the moments in between. These poems and short stories show us that the city is inseparable from its people, and it's the voices of our times which add colour and meaning to the brickwork. But it also shows us that Edinburgh is still a great source of inspiration for its inhabitants and those who pass through it; it takes them on journeys, through which the people and the city are forever altered.

Russell Jones and Claire Askew

Ways in

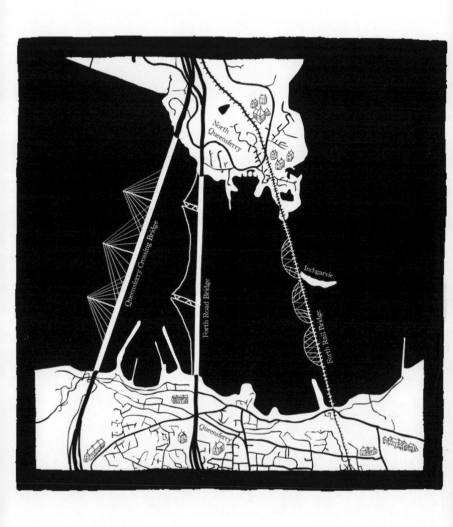

A Firmament

Edinburgh

Marianne Boruch

To remember. Because we don't do that
quite right in America. Edinburgh! Where impatience
wore down patience, our waiting in rain or the about
to rain. But a lull between darkest sky and shiny
moss-glorious trees, whatever wild neglected garden
seen from the street, my favorite kind of beauty.

Enough said, I guess. All the alas and what not
in that city. A few graves, an iron gate
as we stood there, and our bus
flares up, stops, wheezing open its doors near an old
was-it-a-church? Same late afternoon, same
sepia light, stones mortared with smaller stones to
finish a wall in gloom so far
gone ago. The ordinary *is* strange—
duh!—a mash-up.
Zone *then*. Zone *now*. Zone *everlasting*, any century
workmen calling it quits, stalking off
for a pint and bangers and mash, more of this world
than sorrow.

Well. Which is to say we were
up that double decker in a flash, at one with mouthy
punks lip-pierced, at one
with the oldest, most elegantly scarved ladies
buttoned up to the throat. Home to
supper like everyone else,
time travel and lens. Sweet damn!
be damned.

I wish a specific corner came to mind but the months
and months since have their own blank and vivid
business to forget.
It's gone or I'm gone, we were or never were
is the thing.

The place I mean might be
just down from Waverley or closer to the flat
on Strathearn, a kitchen we loved, our pull on the rope
until laundry filled the upper quadrant of the room,
and behind a sprawl of shirts,
socks strung up to dry, we stared out
distant, that observatory, that hill: *we should
go sometime.* Starry bits named or not and which one—
Light years burn up there.

A gate, a street, a shrug, wide lull in the heavens.
And future past
a verb tense to be invented yet.

Island

Inchcolm Island

Jonathan Bay

The seagull is tone deaf;
a blurt, a blast,
nothing but mess,
these rough bluffs
smacked by waves,
and seals, and the cough
of calls loud enough
to drown this choir
belting in the cracked abbey.

If the gulls are a bell,
a tinkle of metal,
turn them to doves
and pray over their white
bird bones, angels
calling to Columba.

Sea Legs
Forth Road Bridge

Dave Coates

Maybe that's all that there is.
Maybe you run through the streets
along roads over bridges on railway
lines flown over cathedral
towns lit up all blue green like swamp
mushrooms like coral like Christmas tree
lights like the Forth Road Bridge a frame
above night-bound trawlers crossing tra
la finding your sea legs cut shadows
in the sky far below the feet of one
on the moon-blackened bridge
regarding all that there is.

Drifting Off, Blackness Castle Car Park
Blackness Castle

Jane McKie

Fife's coastal scroll
            dusted in charcoal
                 curtain wall falling
its watermark self
           carried downstream:
                 I wake a whole nation
a whole readied fleet
           insomnia machines
                 to ferry back the stones

At The New Forth Crossing

The Forth Bridges

Sally Evans

It may be we prefer
these flying roads
that overcome the sea
and give views of the country,

the rail bridge mighty,
making the trains look small,
built in the wake
of failure on the Tay,

road bridge, fifty years back
built under-strength
so now men dig and raise
a replacement,

new road sections south
sending our Sat Navs out
into the long dark grass
confused by ignorance,

where, though we know we are
overlooking Dunfermline,
we'll soon choose to return
to the squares of the town

whose bridges bridge a loch
that has long gone
where geese still land
horses pull no hard load.

Rock lover leaving ritual
South Queensferry

Iain Morrison

Passing the trip on Grindr
on the train
reminding me of when

the European faces
two-tiered
in curious languages

stacked up
set out to me
but I didn't come back that way.

Whistle
stop why not
as a package tour

Dalmeny, many misses of you
because of when you were here
At Dalmeny. Station

crawful of emptied silence
only being
back-filled

the memento rock
inferring a hole
in my Delft left pocket.

At the shore
ghoster
tidy returns

Your presence
along coasted ahead
and always insistent backnote.

Who passed just now
would have seen us
walk.

A step returning the rock
ringed emotion
in place I am swept for

Hand location-based to loosen
and not clench
around the space laboratory of it.

Smoke, pass same factory building
plainly symbolise
pain.

The Forth sucks off
the family shoes
I shed

in this calmed cyclical
supportive piers go up
not quite under my chassis.

A rock swap?
How an attractive boy walks
by I wish to be walking into

arm smells
woody here
and a bit fewer

But
rain homing
a humming I'd forgotten in now

to the rocks
to the choice made
not to progress

Where the pipeline is
keep walking
grass and wrack

the same ground given
over thresholds of nicotine
sickness no weed to share with you.

Sorry for the ash in your rockpool,
my gentle man walking,
my mega-fauna.

Rock back
the housing wasn't fitting
undulating blue parallelograms

Throwing to beach
the beachcombed
stone

I thank for you the gods of the gays
and the Scots
and the broader Celts and kelps.

Bear mermaid,
steer on one-line municipal,
don't present with me at the rock depot.

This ended,
and to know it was here, stand
the colour fade of the sand's drying.

Soliton

Canal an Aonaidh

Pàdraig MacAoidh

B'ann air am pios seo de mhac-meanma
Thomas Telford a chunnaic John Scott Russell

an soliton, 'tonn an eadar-theangachaidh',
marbh-shruth a bhris fon bhàt' 's a chum a' dol

na ruith gun lagachadh fad a' chanail.
Lean Russell e, air each, dà mhìle, fad gach

lùb 's car a' chladhain: 'a singular, beautiful
phenomenon' a dh'fhàg, gun teagamh,

a chinnt ann an Newton luaisgte. Mar esan,
tha an t-àite-sa a' faireachdainn seachad air rudeigin,

le cothrom air maireannachd gun iarraidh
ann an saoghal a bha, 's a tha, 's bu chòir a bhith na fhlusg.

Tha gaothan dìthidh stoirm Jonas a' piocadh
a' chanail, pocannan plastaig a' tathaich

nan cuilcean, a' dèanamh cailleach an dùdain.
Tha lachan a' dabhdail thall dhan a' bhruaich eile

air uisge luaineach, a' siubhail bho siar gu sear
gun iùl, agus a' dol ann luath. Gu bràth

cha dèan iad uisge-beath' ann an Lochrin,
às an tug an teine ann an 1801

Soliton

Union Canal

Peter Mackay

It was not beyond the stretch of Thomas Telford's
imagination for John Scott Russell to first see here

the soliton, his 'wave of translation',
a wake that broke free from its boat and hurried on,

running the length of the canal without weakening.
Two miles Russell tracked it on horseback,

along the 'windings of the channel': a 'singular,
beautiful phenomenon' that must have shaken

his certainty in Newton. Like him, the place feels post-
something, a new-found possibility of permanence

in a world where all was, is, should be, flux.
The last winds of storm Jonas pick the canal;

plastic bags ghost in and out of the reeds;
ducks scut to the opposite banks across

water that, restless, from west to east
is going nowhere, quick. Never again

will they make whisky in Lochrin
where the fire in 1801 carried the smell

of burning malt from the distillery
to the mills of Balerno, the farmworkers

às an tug an teine ann an 1801
fàileadh brach' air losgadh on taigh-stail'
gu muileann Bhaile Àirneach 's mànas Niddrie Mains.

Gu bràth cha gheàrr na sgalagan an coirce
dhan adag misgte mu dheireadh.

Tha na muilnean 's am mànas 's an taigh-charbadan
uile nam flataichean: breigichean dearg maol

a leigeas a-steach an t-uisge. Cha neònach e.
Thig caochladh air gach cùis. Tha soidhne *Virgin Active*

a' priobadh air, ar tighearnan coma a' criomadh air falbh.
Taobh a-muigh, air na clachan-càsaidh

tha bhana geal a' stad, a' tilleadh 's a' teicheadh.
(Gidheadh, ann an dlùth-chomann dùr air choireigin,

tha an ceàrdach 2-bit an ath-dhorais
a' cumail a' dol gu suarach a' gliongadh).

of Niddrie Mains. Never again will those serfs
cut the barley to the last drunken stook.

Those mills and farms are flats, so too the carriageworks,
blunt conversions whose bricks let in the rain.

Evertheless, all must change. The *Virgin Active* sign pricks up,
our flying fucks scoot off to pastures new,

on the cobbled-street outside, white vans stop, reverse,
are gone. (And yet in spite of this,

in stubborn somewhat solidarity,
that two-bit fabrication yard clanks cussedly on.)

Her Last Laugh

Edinburgh Airport

Iyad Hayatleh

For Lamees Tayyem

Each time she was traveling alone
I would divide my heart into two halves
half to accompany her there, and half guarding her
                         absence here
and she was doing the same
half stays with me here
and half calls my presence there
and always the four halves unite at the Airport.

For a quarter of a century
we were shadows of each other
reflection of the same mirror
with our joint step, we commenced our journey
from the diaspora of the refugee camp
to the diaspora of the bagpipes country

always together
always into the soul of each other
it just happened

We've never travelled
from this airport together
she used to go alone,
and I would welcome her back with a bunch
of love. I traveled only once,
she welcomed me back with a river of kisses

Then she departed lonely on her own
and I sealed my goodbye to her with a flood of tears

And now as I travel back and forth
back and forth
no roses anymore
no kisses anymore
just the echo of her last laugh.

Bonny Fie Dee Travellers

Edinburgh Waverley

Sandy Thomson

Arlene was a boakey kid. Anytime she was tipped off her x-y axis she was likely to land her last half-digested meal in the lap of whichever adult was scrubbing her face clean with a hankie or dragging her along by the arm. Other things set her off too. The path of the telegraph line spooling past the back window of the car.

Swoop. Swoop.

That would do it. Something about the way it sagged down then got hitched up like a dragging school sock by the pylon. Over and over and over and blaaaaaaah.

Family legend had it that she threw up in the hood of her dad's parka once, when he was driving.

I told you I needed out Dad.

This time the thrum of the wheels under her seat on the train had vibrated its way up through her legs and bum. It got into her low-down belly and though she'd fought it and done all the breathing, it had crept into her high-up belly. Her high-up belly was already twitchy – like somebody waiting to get tickled. Arlene couldn't spell bronchial asthma but she'd had it since she was two. She'd been wheezy last night. Mum had given her two spoonfuls of medicine in the early hours of the morning and she'd woken at breakfast time with her hands shaking and her eyes all juddery. Mum said it was adrenalin. She couldn't spell adrenalin either. And she could never eat her toast when she had the mediciney shakes.

The train had went thrumrumthrumrumthrumrum until she was fighting sickness off in waves. If she was jostled getting into her coat or dunted on the way off the train she'd coup. But

Paw Paw and Pom Pom walked her carefully into Waverley's main thoroughfare, one of them on either side. Paw Paw's big hand between her shoulders. Her cousin Rhona rolled her eyes and called her a jessie but then she strode in front of the three of them pretending to be the Green Cross man, with her hands on her hips and her legs wide apart like a big X, putting a policeman hand up to folk in their path to stop them coming near, even grown-ups.

Stop! Look! Listen! she told them.

Pom Pom told her to stop.

In an American accent, Rhona said I'm a Handful ma'am. Just doin' ma jawb.

Rhona was always a Handful and she was absolutely positively a Handful today. She was excited to be in Edinburgh. Her and Arlene were both double double excited to be there without their Mums or Dads.

Paw Paw and Pom Pom would stop at good windows. They would let you have all the cakes from the top of the cake stand before having bread and butter from the bottom bit. They would buy you things without making you save up for some of it, so you knew the value of money. They didn't make you help out with dishes to earn it, or get something for your wee brother or sister so they didn't feel left out.

Paw Paw and Pom Pom just bought you stuff because you fancied it.

Arlene's Mum and Rhona's Mum both said when they were out with Paw Paw and Pom Pom they were Spoilt Ruined.

Rhona bounced up and down in the middle of the busy station. She pulled the hood of her anorak up and hauled at the cords around until it shut like a fishing net and her nose stuck out the tiny wee hole. She wiggled her body and shot her feet out in an excited tap dance.

Arlene felt a bit better. Pom Pom was going to get her a hat. And a scarf. And maybe some gloves if they saw something that went.

It was much colder than Carnoustie.

Rhona puffed air out her mouth. It made smoke.

Arlene! Arlene look! I'm a train!

Pom Pom rolled her eyes.

You're a blether, Paw Paw said. Here. Better no waste a good reek, and gave her an unlit Capstan Full Strength out his packet.

Rhona posed like Diana Dors, sucking on the fag and blowing a sigh of steam out of her mouth.

My eye but I was needing that, she said, the exact same way Pom Pom did when she sat down at the kitchen table after cleaning the house. Pom Pom flicked her hand out and skiffed her on the back of the head.

Paw Paw's laugh was so like Muttley the Dog on Stop That Pigeon it made Arlene's asthma hurt just hearing it. Heh heh heh heh

Dinnae encourage her John.

Arlene looked up past Pom Pom's red winter hat. Up and more up. Like a circus tent. So high. She could almost see a sparkly lady on a swing up there. Between the grey struts and arches of iron. Swoop. Swoop. Oh no. Don't swoop. Don't boak.

Arlene's dad worked at the Foundry Ironworks. He poured boiling hot metal into casts to make things like the station roof. Little girls weren't allowed in the foundry but one day when she was big enough he would take her to the Supervisor's window so she could look down and see the fire and the lava and the sparks.

The station sounded like the foundry too. Waves of noise. Loudspeakers going wah, wah and not really words. Banging and whistles. People all busy.

She saw a pigeon fetutter down from the ceiling. A ravel of feathers. It stole a biscuit right out a wee boy's hand.

Her head got yanked to the side when Rhona pulled her hood. She breathed more hot puffs of steam in Arlene's ear.

We're in Edinburgh!

I know! she whispered back.

Ladies and Gentlemen! – The Amazing Arlene and Rhona are Going To The Big Shops! Thrills and Spills Ladies and Gentlemen! Thriiiiills and Spiiiiills!

Rhona was a big fan of Evel Knievel.

C'mon you Gigglers. Pom Pom was wrapping her red scarf around her neck almost up to her lipstick. We've to get to Markies. 'Mon

Paw Paw said, Is that the direction you're heading? Princes Street?

Aye. The lassies need woolies.

Right. Right ye are.

What?

Arlene and Rhona are in Paw Paw's coat pocket looking for his poke of liquorice bullets.

Well, I mentioned to Davey I'd be in toon. There's the Vittlers next week and he wants to talk to me aforehand. I thoucht I'd maybe nick up and see him, seeing as we're here.

John—

The Vittlers were boring. Paw Paw and Uncle Ally had a pub. On the wall of their pub was a certificate in a frame saying John Anderson Strachan and Alasdair Littlejohn Strachan were Scottish Licensed Victuallers. It meant they'd passed a test to be a good person from the Licensing Board. They could sell liquor.

Liquor.

Like in a cowboy saloon.

Every time the licensing board was due, and a lot of times when it wasn't, there was a Vittler meeting. Sometimes they had Vittler meetings even on holidays. Vittlers today was Bad.

The girls stood together silently, being Very Good. Arlene's stomach twisted on the inside.

The golden day of cakes and treats and hats and scarves in Markies could disappear like steam if Paw Paw was meeting a Vittler. The Vittlers all smelled of gin and whisky and fag reek. They laughed really loud and pinched your cheeks too hard. And they spoke for ages and ages, waving their glass or their fag about, while you made one packet of crisps and a lemonade last forever.

Pom Pom was moving her mouth like she was trying to get toffee off her false teeth.

Paw Paw put on his bunnet. Och cheer up Clara. Bona fide travellers and aw that. I'll no be all day.

He looked down at Arlene, the word gannet. Always asking if she didn't know because that's what she'd been telt to do.

We're travellers she said.

We are that

We came from Carnoustie just now.

We did

What's bonny fie dee Paw Paw?

Well, it's French Ah think. It means real. Real honest to God travellers.

Like us?

Just like us. And do you know what? It used to be that you couldnae get a drink on a Sunday in Scotland unless you were a bona fide traveller and had come at least 3 and half mile for it. Is that no awful?

Aye

Imagine that eh?

Rhona said, Could you get water?

Oh aye. But you couldnae get a drink drink.

Pom Pom was a dark floating cloud of silence somewhere above their heads. She grabbed their nearest shoulder a bit more firmly than it needed. They were too big to run away. Her handbag slid down her arm and dunted Rhona.

Right you two. Princes Street. Up aw those steps.

Now haud on, said Paw Paw

What? What for? What would we haud on for? Pom Pom said.

Paw Paw smacked his pockets, checking for his wallet as if he was a wee bit worried it might have crawled off and hidden somewhere. Then he went, Ah! when he found it where it always was. He took out a note, folded it along its length and, looking Arlene in the eye, he raised an eyebrow and offered it to her from between his middle and his pointing finger. For all the world like a gambler buying more chips from the dealer in a casino.

Arlene took it and said Thank you very quietly

John. That's far too much.

Och now.

He looked at the lassies

That's for sharing, he said. Then he was John Wayne. Straight down the middle pardners, ya hear?

Rhona said Thank you Paw Paw and flung herself around his waist.

Pom Pom tuts. Grabs Rhona's hand.

C'mon. Arlene put that away where you won't lose it for Chrissake.

She takes Arlene's other hand and they move through the people to the foot of the steps up to Princes Street and Markies and the woolly hats.

They hear Paw Paw in the crowd over the wah wah speaker and the bangs and the whistles, shouting cheerfully he'll see them back at the train.

Pom Pom's shiny black clumpy heels hit the stone floor like a flamenco dancer and they run skip to keep up.

The steps are steep like a mountain. Really really like a mountain. Arlene would like a rope round her waist tied to Pom Pom up ahead. There's a postcard of blue and white sky in the distance, way at the top. The steps don't match. Some are concrete. Some are made of shiny stuff with sparkly bits in, like the floor of the station. Some are disgusting and slidey and mossy green and made of gravestone stone. Some are broken. The crush of people bounce off the lassies and keep forcing them to let go of the hand rail. Rhona says Hey! Mind out! and walks in front of Arlene saying 'Scuse me, 'scuse me to folk coming toward them until Pom Pom tells her to stop her nonsense.

They lift their feet nearly waist high it feels like. Giant steps. Feeling the promise of Princes Street and the blue white fresh air in front of them and the deep open mouth of the station falling away behind. Wah wah. Wah wah.

The smells change in gusts and puffs. Macaroni and cheese, pipe smoke, aftershave, wet metally steam, mould. They're about halfway up when Arlene gets a whiff of the sick in a corner and just like that she's boakey again.

Pom Pom! Pom Pom I'm gonna be sick!

In one movement Pom Pom gathers Arlene's hair back out the way and spins her to face the wall. She stands behind her and puts an arm round the bairn's waist, lifting her up and away from the splattery mess she's making and holding her clear until she's done.

Then she puts her down well out the way of it all and takes out a pile of hankies. Pom Pom's mouth goes like a pulled thread while she scrubs Arlene's face clean and checks her front for mess.

Better?

Uh-huh. I'm sorry. I had to.

It's awright chickie. No harm done.

Pom Pom pats her on the bum twice and hooks her handbag hand into Rhona's.

C'mon you two. Onward and upwards.

The hat she got was amazing. Like a big blue squashy strawberry.

Craigmillar

Craigmillar

Dorothy Lawrenson

A single magpie struts in the quiet street
where the scheme peters into the park. I stop
on the path, look back at the tower blocks:
grey gatekeepers between this foreground hush
and the rush of the city, in the northern distance
Arthur's Seat a gorse-embroidered backcloth.

The woods, once a dazzling tapestry of hawk,
horse and hound, are now patrolled by joggers
and dogwalkers. I reach the defensive doocot
that launched birds from its turret, musket balls
from its gunloops. In the courtyard, two yew trees
more stoic than stone, an eroded coat-of-arms
on the wall mouthing like a crestfallen queen
I am but a body whose heart's torn away.

In an upstairs bedchamber, a jackdaw's nest
makes a mock of the fireplace. I retreat to walk
in the grounds, as far as the sitooterie of rusty
corrugated iron in its grove of blackthorn, creamy
lace ornamenting the leafless black spines,
a magpie hopping over cracked tarmac.

North

Dwam

Dean Village

Jane Yolen

My own Brigadoon, hidden
not by mists but by traffic
racing along Queensferry Road,
that rush like loosed arrows
into the heart of the old town.

I stumbled into the dwam,
following the river's ramble,
past old millstones, remnants
of lives before mine ever began,
greener than I could have known.

What leads us into, out of dreams?
How was I so touched without a finger
laid against the fragile shield of skin,
that pulsing along the ley lines
of my wakening heart?

No answer except I found my lost
past that morning, an oasis,
start of many walking poems,
like this one, stepping out alone
along the Water of Leith.

Uisce beatha

The Water of Leith

Anne Connolly

This homophonic water needs no boatman. No fee.
For it is uisce beatha all the way to the sea.
A running of rocks.
A tangle of trees
knotted to the banks.
A halt for Mister Heron who waits Confucian, an ageless
silk-screen print who knows his tide will turn.

Worn thin and less befeathered than he was before
he has perfected still life, just by the steps that lead
to Modern Art.
He reflects on the pool
where it widens out
before the rapid rush.
And loved ones stigmatized before by old ignorance
are remembered here on wrought-iron bench and stone
and a gathering of hearts.

Mallards catch the spring drift, watch their new brood
learn the splash and float and paddle. The dipping curiosity
and thrill of weed and worm.
The thwack of tennis back
and forth on the far side
accompanies the summer pech and grunt of Murray
aspiration. And under Mr Telford's bridge there is
a quernstone, gritty with the memory of grain.

Ignored by joggers and the cyclists sleek with lycra
on their ride to work, tourists ooh and aah, enchanted
with this unexpected winding wilderness. Tended
and tamed, but not
too often or too much.
Each stroll is singular.
Paved with autumn, crisped with frost or squelched
with an excess of rain. Today the path and its companion
snake unruly.

But there is a melting in this March-bound air that irrigates
the city's breath. Catches sun-shafts, the flicker-dance
of rising light which
etches pale shadows.
Celandines are stirring.
Hordes of bluebells will soon begin to read the score
that dangles every note of their being. And moon-flecks
will foam the sea as she is drawn in to meet
the kindred longing of water.

Uisce beatha – The water of life (Gaeilge)

Secret Garden

Dean Street Gardens

Janette Ayachi

A place where the play park has a sand-pit
and the gates are groomed for secret keys.
Where grandparents walk teenagers in circles,
mothers unhinge over fences
eating air and lifting litter.
Apologies and singing children,
a hair-band in absentia on a plateau of grass
and a picnic bench under a liquid canopy of trees.
The clouds hover like gulls over a ghost ship
as if there is always mist to hide in.

Children all crave to be seen;
they destroy sand castles too quickly,
tiny toddlers stamping giant footprints.
Mum I made a hole, then the hole disappeared!
Only the moats remain curving their smiles
through a thicket of Trafalgar-red spades.
Freddie turns a spade into a wand
then turns me into a bear.
Gilbert spills his blueberries, stares at the splatter
as if he were watching them grow.

A man practises chanter-song as he walks his pliant dog
tapping the sheet music with his wedding ring;
and when a playgroup bursts over the horizon
like alien invaders shrouded in neon,
it is only the mothers who think them enemies
as we juggle our snacks and our observations,
look at each other like the sun is always in our eyes.

The kids are mostly happy or unhappy;
forging fond memories as they vanish behind bushes
and sometimes smoke, throw stones at spiders,
let ladybirds trapeze-walk across their arms.
And later, when the mothers return home
we watch water boil, feel like magicians ourselves,
clandestine in our midnight veils of moons and stars.

I lock myself in for a while to think:
move the furniture so I can't find the doors or windows,
wear all my keys on chains, all my hearts on mirrors
remembering her stare across the swings,
the lust slashed visible through the domestic solidarity.
Our bond of motherhood – a mound of Lionesses,
her eyes waxy and dark like Whitby jet
zirconia in the light – more spiced than shadow,
and widening to accept my smile
as love arrived in stealth.

Making Bubbles outside the Modern Art Gallery

National Gallery of Modern Art

Aiko Greig

(after Martin Creed's No. 975)

We have been entrusted to watch this bright light
for the afternoon. We have toured all the art,
and now, on the parkland stoop of Modern Two,
you unpack in plain sight: a box of snacks,
a loop of string, a dish, our own soap mix.

You dip the string into the soap while our niece
eats tiny sandwiches. You make the first bubble,
huge as a person, iridescent rainbows of colour,
a column of diamonds floating skyward. She stops
mid-bite, a fleck of egg cress still in her mouth

as she gapes at your creation. She is sparkling
like a bubble, wants to make one with you,
her small hands soaked with soap suds, clutching
the string. Where do bubbles come from?
Can I fit inside? Where does it go when it floats

past the trees? We return to our car, our clothes
and hands slick and soap-tacky. We are no good
at this, but in the rearview as we leave, beyond
the girl asleep in the back seat, a blue neon light
glows: EVERYTHING IS GOING TO BE ALRIGHT

Save A Red, Eat A Grey

Stockbridge Market

Lauren Pope

It's all I can do
not to wag a finger
through the air,
but then I picture Ahmedi
lifting the rat's heart
off the floor in Nacala.

I turn to Elsa
for French foodie wisdom –
schooled in the art
of outdoor marketing,
always skeptical
except at mealtimes;
but even she looks dubious.

She lights a fag, blows
smoke pointedly
at the purple flesh –
With enough sauce…
her nasal voice lifting
at the end like a hook.

The Charity Shops of Stockbridge

Stockbridge

Jane Griffiths

                    The Charity Shops of Stockbridge
each Saturday
               invite you to shelter or save
                          a snowing globe
a case of ammonites
                  not from local stone
                        a jar of marbles
and an Indian mirror
                 shuttered and barred
                           as if reflections
were winged
              item a pair of glass earrings
                          cherry-formed
items an ostrich feather
               a painted stool
                    a boy's own satchel
a necklace
            ostensibly amethyst and pearl
                       a corduroy skirt
a shovel
           a stopped clock, repeatedly
                   a book of words
for music,
          perhaps
               a complete run of Vanity Fair
item a loose grey cardigan,
               in its pocket
                     a painted bird

items a box of spice jars
                              some doll's house stairs
                                                        a tapestry kit
to stitch something loosely
                              that loosely
                                                resembles the bridge
you cross each Saturday
                            with these makings
                                                    of a tenement
or fingerhold
                    on the sky stretched grey
                                                above the shared
laundry line lifting
                          in the wind that is home
                                                        and away

Gabriel's Road

Stockbridge

Hamish Whyte

Gabriel's Road isn't
   a road:
there's steep steps
   you could break
your neck on
and a walled lane
   you could have a huff in –
but the main thing is
   it's a short cut
(Edinburgh's a city
   of short cuts)
heaven either way.

friday nights in Kay's have changed
Kay's Bar

nick-e melville

we won't get a free drink this new year
now we're no longer pillars of the bar
we've missed this

the gold escutcheons on the red
we'd never noticed
before

the old guy   always reading
with half a guinness
and port chaser

lunch   which
we've never tried

the old fire burned
black with soot

the other old guy
in the arran jumper

the time some young woman
snogging his face off at the bar
almost jumped his old bones

THE GLENLIVET & ISLAY SPIRIT
SUCCESSORS TO JOHN KAY.
we didn't miss some boring guy
we don't recognise

going on about burgers
you canny beat a homemade burger
took a bit of work
onion on top
you get the gherkins and mustard
if it's no meat
it's no a burger
friday nights in Kay's have changed
some other guy says

in the other room
                our wee annexe
the little round table
where we used to sit
is broken
now a wrought iron leg half cut

at the other table
where we used to sit
from time to time
two men talk about stocks

and that would be the end of us

in here are the books
Encylopedia and Children's Britannica
pub guides   RISK
the world conquest game
Chambers' SLANG dictionary
and   bizarrely
Céline's *Journey to the End of the Night*
Calder edition
It's FREE!
it's FUN!

I'll give it to Calum
he wants to read some prose   being fed
up with poetry
          the karma of literature

The faux old   'Billiard Match' prints

"LEFT"
"KISS"
"SNOOKERED"
"THE CANON"

then there's the pictures of Jamaica Street
in the 60s   as slum
before the mews

Making Love in Ferns

Royal Botanic Garden Edinburgh

JL Williams

Children and foxes race through the gardens at night.
They close their eyes and run, using scent to guide each step.
The boys and girls hold hands. The magnolias flap their hands.
Monkey puzzle trees waggle their hundred, hundred tails.

The peonies raise their mille-feuille organza,
night bees dangle from under their ruched skirts.
The bamboo shivers. The coots leap up on skeleton feet.
In the glasshouses huge black moths unfurl velvet wings.

No one makes a sound.
The wind holds her gaspy breath.
The Chinese waterfall pauses
as if it were glass stretched.

Tomorrow no one will have the slightest clue
how you and I spent the whole night through.

Mela

Leith Links

Esa Aldegheri

The air is ribbons
of spices, chips, henna, suncream,
seagulls, bhangra, voices
in different languages that echo

my call, the cry of the outrun parent –
"Piano, tesoro, aspetta!"
"Slow down, darling, wait!" –
 as children spot the candyfloss and pelt

into the path of a man with a bike who spits,
"If you can't control your children
take them back to where you came from!"
all rage and compensatory lycra.

Later, faces full of sugar and sunshine,
we lie on Leith Links and I try to imagine
needing to squash all the lives of this city
into angry belonging

while the sea-wind blows from the North,
while the bones of the plague-dead rest beneath
the Edinburgh Mela unfurling around
our children's laughter.

West

Animals
Edinburgh Zoo

Theresa Muñoz

like lions   we raised our heads on the hill
the day we married above Edinburgh's zoo
like swans we paired for life
like wolves we trusted   like squirrels we saved
like peacocks we dressed in high pomp
purple streaks above my eyes   like tiger stripes
your silk tie shiny as an otter's pelt
like a doe I stepped on light feet
your tearful eyes   like an owl's sinking gaze

like meerkats   our guests tiptoed in a half arc
embracing the day   noon light   our vows
like parrots we recited   like elephants we wept
like penguins we promised to come back
our kiss was wet & we nuzzled necks
to the banging joy of the crowd

like gazelles we raced down the carpet
velvet red like animal tongues
like rabbits   we reached the end & turned round
like monkeys   we lifted our palms for rain
you slung your jacket over my shoulders
it smelled of you completely & fitted like a skin

like honeybees we danced   like hippos we gorged
like pigeons we homed   to our sea-facing house
like camels we cast long shadows
like lions we lay down

Vanishing Points

Corstorphine

Andrew J. Wilson

a cloud of frogspawn
in glacial meltwater –
this place has no name

Coriestiorfionn
a hollow in a wet place –
milk-white meadowsweet

Corsturrpenn stockade
a fold on a rough round hill –
ticks in the wolf's pelt

Thorfinnr's Crossing –
a twelve-point stag vanishes
between the two lochs

the Cross of Torfin –
a filigree of lichen
in the Celtic knot

Crostorfin village –
under the nose of a cat
an owl takes a rat

Corstorphin Doocot –
in the empty pigeonholes
spiders spin their webs

on Corstorphine Hill –
a runaway wallaby
waits at the bus stop

#corstorphine –
foraging for takeaway
a three-legged fox

Kursturvun free port –
long-drained lochs fill up again
as the ice caps melt

this place has no name –
the spawn of the tongue-twisters
are lost to the stars

Amphitheatre

Murrayfield

Andy Jackson

Flowers are in bloom again, masses flowing
past the orphaned clock, through the gates
and up the stairs, dripping February rain.
I came here for the noble drama of the war,
the lightning two-act play, the ceilidh birl
and set, part majesty, part butchery.
Here is the taut ensemble down below,
still giants, even from the highest gallery;
the pudding-headed pachyderms, all gum
and solid sinew; the sugar-crusted feet
and spotless kit of supple ballerinos
wary of the touchline and its precipice;
the gimlet-eyed professor, surfacing from
rucks of fle sh with his hunk of meat –
the bladder/ball – the perfect plot device.

Down at stageside you can hear the snarl
and champing of the two front rows,
see the nostrils purged of steam and snot,
smell the black arts in the unlit mine
of the scrum. Then the ball comes loose, alive
and dancing through a dozen pairs of hands,
unshackled from the script to improvise its end.
Up here in the roaring stand it all plays out
in high-def; the pauses while the pails of blood
are emptied, passages of *pas de basque*
and *Grand Guignol*. The chief protagonist

emerges from the wings, fists like gnarls,
waiting for his chance to influence the plot
praying life will, just for once, offload
a good clean ball, open up a clear run to the line.

Zen & the Scottish Long-Ball Game
Tynecastle

Roddy Shippin

It's after about an hour
when the dog hairs start to unravel
and the lower back-ache starts to spread.

We're forty minutes from the next pint –
both sets of fans have choired
all the Sloop John B-tuned witticisms we
can muster for now, amongst a limp
recession of union jacks.

After an early frenzy, the ball
has barely acknowledged either line;
both teams have been repeatedly encouraged
to *GET* or – *'MON* tae *fuck*, with little effect.

The linesman has stoically outlasted Euan's vocal chords,
the bald man two rows behind is tearing up
his coupon – lamenting *Saint FUCKING Johnstone'*s

inability to keep *a clean FUCKING sheet* against *Ross
FUCKING County,*
while his all-over seared-maroon skin tone
is either a mark of loyalty, frustration
or lack of sun cream. Willie, Hannah & Michael are off for pies.

Duffin has slipped into twitter.

The patched, steaming ranks are bursting
for a granted release –
a swept-up net of songs & limbs
                I nearly miss
the full-back inching out of his box – a hoof
swinging the ball skyward

to arc through seagulls & clouds
with everything scattered below

The Diggers, Hogmanay

Diggers | Athletic Arms

Nancy Somerville

Therr's a giant compass oan the flerr
– mibbe aw roads lead fae here,
ma local,
where the barstaff ken ma name
an ma tipple o choice.

This is wherr they gaither:
the grizzled coallie dug sidlin in
unner yir table, moochin fir crisps;
Billy, wi his pint o 80 shillin an his paper;
the doms team an thir challengers
chappin an cheerin as the pieces fa.
Therr's the resident scrievers, the pensioners,
the Jambos (we're in spittin distance o Tynecastle)
the secret Hibbees, students, tourists,
mibbe a cooncillor, an MSP or twa
an aw the rest,
listnin tae the music o the fiddlers an penny-whistlers
spillin oot fae the back room.

Thenight therr's even a piper,
an the talk is o the year past,
a bad yin for maist bi aw accoonts,
an resolutions fir the wan tae come.
The young yins beside us
buck the trend, discussin hamsters,
an whit sweeties they ett when they wir wee,

while the ghost o auld Jimmy
sits in the coarner,
wi his book,
quiet as aye

then they crood in,
the loved yins we've missed lang since,
an some fae jist the ither day,
aw gaithered roon tae toast wi us
this liminal time.

A Man's a Man for A' That

Lothian Road

Douglas Bruton

Nobody don't pay him no heed. Not unless it's to look away or to quicken their step, or maybe to cross to the other side of Lothian Road like they was on the wrong side all along – some of them do that.

Nobody looking at him, unless it's the little girl holding onto her mammy's hand, and her hair's in tight pigtails, and she's knee high to a grasshopper, and from behind her mammy's coat-tails she dares to peek. And the girl knows it's rude to stare, been told often enough, but she does it anyway – stares at the man with his hair all shocked and tangled and torn, and his hoddin gray army coat that's seen better days, reaching almost to the ground and it's tied closed with old string, and his scuffed forever-lost-their-shine boots tied just the same. And he smiles, doesn't he now, and his smile is broken and gap-toothed and black, but it is a smile all the same and so the little girl gives him back an uncertain smile of her own.

The man, old as hills or history books, holds a plastic cup in one hand, reaching for pennies, or pounds if he's in luck. He shakes it to show how little he has and it makes a music of sorts. And the girl, well, hasn't she a penny in her pocket? And she wants to add it to his music, but her mammy pulls her quickly near and then as quickly away without looking at the man.

His name is Tam. He peers up at the blue of the sky, so blue it almost hurts, and Tam's face is lifted like he might be an Old Testament prophet speaking with God, and he says a prayer of sorts and counts his blessings, such as they are. It is not cold today and it is not wet and the air is still instead of sting. In his cup he calculates he has enough already for a cup of tea, hot and with a wee drop milk and two heaped sugars thank you dear, and a bit of change left over. Maybe the woman in the take-out coffee shop will feel sorry for him and he'll get a sandwich with his tea. Her name's Kitty and her bark is worse than her bite.

Down at the bottom of the road, close enough he can hear the bells of the new trams, and there's a man standing in front of the Carlton Hotel. He's maybe as tall as a door and as broad, and he holds himself stiff and straight. He wears a hat with a glassy peak like something an officer in the army might wear. And his maroon coloured coat is edged with yellow braid and the buttons are brassy like gowd, and he's got white gloves on his hands, pure and white as nurses' aprons.

''Morning, Tam,' he says, and he touches the peak of his cap, touching with the pinch of finger and thumb of one hand. Like a salute it is, or like he might be about to remove the hat or tip it, but just touching and then dropping his hand fast to his side again. 'How's it going?' he says.

Tam holds his arms out wide, as he would if he was about to embrace the doorman or the whole world, and he turns in a shuffling and imperfect circle, and his smile is as full as his smile can be, and his eyes glint.

The doorman of the Carlton Hotel nods and he laughs. Then he puts one hand into the deep pocket of his coat and he pulls out a spilling handful of change. It is all copper and bit silver. He leans towards Tam and lets the money slide from his palm into Tam's cup.

'You go canny now, see,' the doorman says, and he winks at Tam. Then, remembering his place, he darts forward, quick and easy, and he opens the door of a taxi that has just pulled up, and he helps out a woman in fine clothes, her silken hair all bobbed and bowed, and the tinsel show of rings on all her fingers – and who knows, maybe on her toes, too.

The doorman takes the woman's bag, waves the taxi away imperiously, and ushers the woman protectively towards the entrance of the hotel, passing some sweet nothing pleasantry with her about the day and formally welcoming the woman to the Carlton Hotel, Edinburgh.

Tam shakes his cup. The music is a little heavier now and he feels certain he has enough for a sandwich with his cup of tea, even if Kitty at the shop is in a surly and sullen mood. He spins in a circle again, his arms flung out like he could be in flight. A pigeon, blood in its eye and startled by Tam's pirouette, takes to the sudden and ruffled air.

Tam checks the time on the fancy clock on the corner of Frasers. It didn't used to be called Frasers. It had a different name before but he can't now remember what that was even though he met a girl there once, outside the shop, on a Saturday closing-time-night, and the street lit up yellow, and it was an arrangement they had – it was an arrangement a lot of young men had with their girls back then. Tam was to take his girl to the pictures but her bus was late and so they went for a drink at The Rutland instead. She drank Babycham bubbles out of a champagne glass and he had a pint of heavy and the man behind the bar winked at him and grinned as if they was friends.

The clock says it's past ten. Tam tips half the money out of his cup and pockets it. He knows it does no good to be shaking a full cup, that no one's going to give him pennies or pounds if his cup looks like he has enough to be going on with. He turns on his heel and heads back up Lothian Road, feeling the pull.

There's the Usher Hall now with its dome all green and pretty. And it's different these days. They've done it up modern with a great glass box stuck on one side. And the stone's been cleaned up nice when it used to be black as soot or blot. Tam wonders if he could be cleaned up the same and what it would mean if he was. There's a woman at the shelter he has a softness for. Perhaps if he was a bit cleaner she'd kiss him if he dared to ask, or with one hand she'd be stroking his cheek or fiddling in his trouser pockets and not looking for change or keys or cigarettes.

'Do you love me?' she might say, and he'd say he does, he really does.

Tam laughs then and it is the sound of crows calling or a dog barking. He shakes his head and he sets off on his way, walking with some small and new found purpose, for he will take his tea and sandwich to a corner of the Meadows on this fine day. There's a space there that he thinks belongs to him, just as he thinks all of Edinburgh belongs to him, and why does it not? From his place on the Meadows he can see the castle above the buildings where the hospital used to be, and off to one side the crouching and sleeping lion of Arthur's Seat, and everywhere the rolling green slopes of the Meadows with trees reaching to the sky and well-trodden paths criss-crossing the park, all of them going somewhere and nowhere. And seagulls there are, dancing on the close-cropped grass, making a small dishonest thunder under their yellow feet that brings the fearful-of-drowning worms to the surface same as if it was rain that was falling. And daffodils that briefly crowded in corners, nodding their bright and golden heads, have turned over, and Spring coories up to Summer, and children turn gleeful cartwheels across the park, their arms and their legs thrown wide so they could be fallen stars; and Tam stretches out on the grass, lying on his back, like he is in a great bed. He could be anyone then and he could be anywhere.

Once there was a girl lying beside him on the grass, years back now, years on years and too many for counting. He closes his eyes and remembers. He thinks maybe it was the same girl that also drank Babycham bubbles in The Rutland bar – maybe it was another girl. She was helping him learn irregular verbs in German: ist, war, gewesen. He loved her then and he told her as much. The sky was blue, like it is today only more blue, as blue as it only ever is in memory, and the sun was warm on his face.

'Do you?' she said. 'Do you love me?' And there was gentle mockery in her sing-song voice.

Tam rolled over and looked her in the face, pretty as peaches.

'I really do,' he said. And he was in earnest as only the young can be, or maybe also the old when they remember. 'Really I do.'

'Now you do,' she said. 'But come tomorrow...'

Tam did not believe in forever. Not back then. He was just a boy after all and back then he only believed in the here and the now, but he told her again that he loved her and he told her that he would love her for all the tomorrows that might be left to them. She sang the words of a Beatles song, something about getting older and being 64 and would he still be sending her a valentine. Tam said he'd love her then, too, when she was old and he was old and they were both old. She'd laughed.

Tam lies on his back, as rich as any man could be. In one hand he holds a plastic cup of tea with a plastic lid, a wee drop milk and two sugars thank you very much, and in the other hand a ham and cheese sandwich, white bread with butter, cut neat into triangles. With his eyes closed everything is the same – ist, war, gewesen: is, was, and shall be. He hears again the sound of children at play, a dog barking with no bite, and somewhere the ring of a bicycle bell.

She must be near to old now, he thinks, that gently mocking girl, and Tam wonders where she is and he wonders if she thinks of him sometimes. Her name comes to him sudden, and he whispers her name, gives shape to it in breath, so soft that no one else hears, soft as grass whispers.

And about him seagulls dance their timeless dance on the rising and falling slopes, and the stretching-tall trees stand on tiptoe as they always have, arms spread wide to embrace the sky; and somewhere near, so near Tam can hear, another boy tells a different girl that he loves her, he really does, and the girl laughs as they always do, and this time Tam laughs too, and he cries also, and no one notices that he does, or if they do then they look away again thinking the old man maybe drunk or mad or stupid.

Mortar

Cloisters Bar

Dave Coates

(from a line by Edward Thomas)

Their voices fill the street but where are the birds?
watchful in the hedgerows' skirts? parting dirt
and water in the gutters? arranging their wooden networks
above the pub's blocked-up flue, gas-fire,
its blackboard fat with blackout paint,
tidy chalk for today's pints
tomorrow and tomorrow, til the day
the burden of small business is relieved,
the public house returns to clay and wood,
last orders and unrotting words,
the street at peace with a homely sky,
the small birds taking their part-time homes for good –
whatever is forever to a bird?

Ath-thogail na Cloinne

Morrison Street

Màrtainn Mac an t-Saoir

Thig mi dhan sgoil nur coinneimh – carson nach tigeadh? –
latha sam bith, bliadhna sam bith fad deich dhem shaoghal,
sin an còigeamh pàirt dheth!
Bus, trèan, càr,
an-diugh 's e th' agam baidhsagal
ga chuibhleadh suas, mar as dual
an aghaidh rang na sràid' seo

– dhan tug 'Am Moireasdanach' ainm
no a bhaisteadh às a dhèidh,
ge b'e cò a bh' ann: gàidheal, gall no eile?
Eile am pailteas a-nist mu a dhìleib:
Brazil, Bangladesh, An Fhraing,
Sìna, A' Phòlainn is Tìr nan Sauna.

Feumaidh mi bhith faiceallach
gun càraich mi sibh (mas e an dithis agaibh a bhios ann)
le cùram air dìollaid; làmh làidir an tacsa an droma,
mum fàg sinn Crois na Cìse.

Agus tillidh sinn – carson nach tilleadh? – tro
lios tlachdmhor Ghardner's Crescent
is leigidh mi leibh leum a-nuas gu:
sunnd an t-samhraidh
brat an fhoghair
brag a' gheamhraidh
lùths an earraich

Is le cleas bheir sinn a-mach Haymarket
gun stad son suiteis, crisps no an taighe-bhig
is saoil dè mo fhreagairt nuair
a dh'iarras sibh Hot Chocolate – 'Ok, dìreach
aon fhear beag eadarrainn?' – is sinn a' feitheamh
an dòmhalas a' chòmhnaird?
An gèill mi?

Is dè na naidheachdan beaga a bheir sibhse dhomh,
a luaidheannan, mu bhrìgh ur saoghail-se?
An deach sibh a-mach a chluic?
An do leigear leibh peantadh?
Dè an còrr a thachair ma-tà?
'Snack, Dadaidh!'
'Seadh, seadh, snack. Ciamar idir a bha e?'

Latha mar chus san t-sreath dh'fhaodte a ràdh
chanainn fhìn sin tric, ro thric, is ghabhainn
iongnadh nach robh sgoinn orra seachad.

Ach aig 3.15 nuair a dhealaicheas mi ris a' chafaidh
lom, shìtheil, seo
is a choisicheas mi null gu othail raon na sgoile sin,
nach brath bloigh tuilleadh air a sgeul fhada Ghàidhlig
gun luaidh air ur geàrr-eachdraidh innt',
bu mhiann leam dìreach son tiotain
gun ruitheadh sibh mar ur beatha – aig peilear dearg ur beatha
– gam ionnsaigh
is gum fairichinn a-rithist fàileadh ur n-òige is ur neochiontais;
gum biodh ar n-anail fhathast air an aon leagadh.

Re-Collecting the Kids
Morrison Street

Martin MacIntyre

I'll come to school to get you – why wouldn't I? –
any day, any year of ten,
a fifth of my life!
Bus, train, car,
today it's a bike
I'm pushing, as ever,
against the grain of this street

– to which 'The Morrison' gave a name
or was it christened in his memory?
Whoever he was: gael, lowlander or other?
Other aplenty these days in and around his legacy:
Brazil, Bangladesh, France,
China, Poland and Saunaland.

I'll have to be sure
to place you both (if it's the two of you?)
carefully on the saddle; a strong hand supporting back,
before we leave Tollcross.

And we'll return – why wouldn't we? – through
Gardner's Crescent and its attractive little park,
I'll let you leap down to:
summer's bliss
autumn's carpet
winter's clang
spring's kick

By stealth, we'll achieve Haymarket
without stopping for sweets, crisps or the toilet
and, what, I wonder will my answer be when asked
for Hot Chocolate – 'Ok, just one wee one between us?' –
as we brave the throng of the bridge-bound platform?
Will I buckle?

And what bits of news will you give me, my darlings,
on the substance of your world?
Did you go out to play?
Were you allowed to paint?
What else happened, then?
'Snack, Daddy!'
'Oh, yeah, snack. Tell me all about it?'

A day like too many others, one might say
I'd say often, too often, and wonder
at their lethargy.

But at 3.15 when I flee this unadorned, hushed, cafe
and cross to that playground commotion,
which betrays not a trace of its long Gaelic story
never mind your brief history there,
I'd love just for a moment
you to run – at top speed – at your topsest, bestest, speed –
towards me
so I'd feel anew the smell of your innocence;
our breathing to still share the same air.

Wonky
Bruntsfield Links

Colin Will

Like everything else my father made,
the sledge was asymmetric, wonky. Built
from scrap wood and painted red,
it weighed a ton. I pulled it
by the piece of washing line
to the top of Bruntsfield Links,
in one of those snowy winters
we used to have, grabbed
the single handrail and launched
downhill. As always, it pulled to the left,
with a brutal momentum.

By Easter the snow was long gone
and the grass mown short
on the Pitch 'N' Putt course.
We boiled eggs with onion skins
to make the shells yellow,
painted them with Winsor & Newton
colours, rolled them down the Links.
They followed the same curved route
the sledge had taken, the route I took,
left-leaning, following the lie
of the land.

The Umbrellas of Edinburgh

Cameo Cinema

Louise Peterkin

This is what we leave you under plush red rows:
tattered crows cast underfoot, their wiry bones
tucked up inside minus one broken spoke
extended like a corpse's finger …
It's the least we can do. We,
who shake off the drops beneath your cloister
with its Scrabble-board letters,
the carnivalesque kiosk in our peripheral.
We who offer up a soggy ticket at the door and our coin-clean
smell of cold to the aisle. After the refurb
the epic leg room is as novel
as the resiny hallmark of something-on-the-seat is familiar.
Never ever
as warm as the palpebral red would suggest but
it lets you know what you *are*: a cool
monogrammed lighter in a Gumshoe's palm –
the alley slicked black with rain like a camera.
We are braced to open and spark
when the curtains part to a rolling ritual of
Pearl and Dean, coming attractions,
Paramount's dreamy mountain.
Les Parapluies de Cherbourg
blossom like camp roses. Deneuve
looks out wistfully at us through her shop window.
Real as our own memories, we take these images.

And so leave these brollies,
for ushers to shine their torch on, like relics,
to be curated in lost property boxes
before we clatter onto Home Street's liquorice slabs
imperceptibly, irrevocably shifted.

Tollcross twopenneth

Tollcross

Richie McCaffery

(for Tom Johnston)

The traffic-clotted roads of Tollcross
make it a dangerous fording on foot

and there's a toll to pay, a boatman's
obol, which stands at two-pence –

the price of an opinion which you
can find discarded at your feet.

I've seen people generous by accident
(lost change or larger pub measures),

but only ever mean on purpose
and since we are human, well-known

for our skill in cocking things up,
we often forget to live so fallibly,

splairging ourselves around. Instead
we listen to those who created us –

on purpose or by accident and let
them tell us the ways we should live.

Urbanity

Tollcross

Colin Will

City landscapes alter all the time. Time was,
Tollcross was all fields, a boggy hollow
where the burn drained. Now the Lochrin Burn
is a drain, brick-channelled, below the King's Theatre,
unseen, unheard, bubbling away under the pantos,
shows and concerts. Streamside, the valley field
became the Street where I was born.
Leven landowners put up the tenements
and named streets for their Fife estates – Tarvit,
Drumdryan, Home – playgrounds for kick-the-can, or
sent out with a shovel after horses to feed the roses.
There were always horses, from the Bread Street Co-
op, and the police stables in Riego Street.
Few cars post-war, of course – they came later –
apart from Rolls-Royces parked in our street
for the first Festival. Opposite the chip shop
was where Granny and Grandpa babysat me,
so Mum could go out to work. They chuntered away
to each other in their native Doric, but toned it down
for me. And when sugar came off ration, they bought me,
from R.S. McColl's, the 'chocolate beans'
which the years changed to Smarties,
as the city changed around them.

The Dalry Road Piano Showrooms
Dalry Road

Sarah Stewart

They were closing for the day,
the salesgirl said:
off limits, no exceptions, *nae chance,*
but my man had a Southern drawl,
could talk his way into anything.
She waved us through.

I took a baby grand,
white as a new tooth.
Memorised Chopin poured like milk –
until I tripped,
bucking and cantering to the end.
I never liked that bastard extended trill.

The salesgirl smirked.
My cowboy looked diminished.
I struck the minor third
and snuck off the finish.

All that night
it rained, and I traced my mistakes
up and down his spine –
fourth finger, second finger,
third finger. Trill.

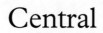
Central

Military Section: Royal College of Surgeons

South Bridge

Aileen Ballantyne

This is the skull with the soft fontanelles
that grew long ago in the womb of a woman
and pushed its way down and was blessed.
These are the sockets of eyes in the face
of a boy who tilled the green field.
Here are the splinters of bone in the hole
where his song spilled out onto grass.

The Night to Come

The Café Royal, West Register Street

Chris Powici

It's a cold half mile from the observatory on Calton Hill
where Thomas Henderson measured out the 20 trillion
                    miles
from Earth to Alpha Centauri
in a six inch lens
but at least I've closed the Café Royal's door
on a bitter east coast wind and – miracle of miracles –
found a window seat by some glad-ragged women
talking of work, husbands and the night to come.

All along the far wall hang Doulton portraits
of dead, brilliant men – Watt, Franklin, Faraday
hunched at their instruments or staring calmly
into space as the light of truth sinks in.

But not Henderson.
Maybe knowing just how lost in space we really are
feels too deep-down-in-the-marrow true
for praise in painted tiles
though when I buy another beer and the barman asks
is that everything?
I think of Thomas at his telescope and want to say
yes everything
except some women talking
the bright window
and beyond these streets and hills
world after world after world

glowing palely in the winter night
just close your eyes, you'll hear
the utter lonesomeness of things
pushing at the door:
the hurt, the heartsick Edinburgh wind.

View of Edinburgh from Calton Hill with the North Bridge and Castle in the Distance

Calton Hill

Jay G Ying

What could be said / for the brun bear rising from that early
East / for there was a clade of life I had not chanced upon / for
my blackish host / for he had not yet risen then to morn / for I
arrived in Heidelberg four days ago / for first to the wild water
I went down / for the heavy bourn of that brackish solitude /
for the brindled fur of a Rhinemaiden in my dream I saw / for
not being a man before I was a translator / for in that anodyne
winter of our silence / for the foreboding wolf I saw slouch
out of the belly of the storm / for the rime on the Rhine's rift /
for the major then / for the minor / for the rain and then / for
folklore's designer / for misfortune's icy lover / for I had said
foreshadowing, I hope it will not snow too hard / for I texted
after I departed, Let me know if you will cross my hearth, but
/ for four days I could not unsee that Old Bridge / for from the
stuck window of his flat I laid my forehead upon / for the first
night he asked me, What is like your hometown / for the cold
Bridge was like the stone arm of his own home / for I could not
forego his bed those days to move on numbed / for the snow /
for his forearm set over mine in bed like a cross / for I dreamt
the neck of the water nicked / for I saw forty last bears sip at it
/ for I could not translate into words / for him / for the reasons
I had come to Heidelberg / for I settled there thinking / for,
Was it not always like this first / for by the last stalled day of
the falling snow's four / for thaw of the sun over the frost / for
I saw a note he had pinned to his fridge / for he had pencilled,
You can use this in the morning / for I will be back late / for as
I sat finally on the train back to Frankfurt in the evening / for

how was I to know years later I would find Turner in January in Edinburgh / for I had not thought much about Heidelberg until then / for it rose back to the surface like a block of ice / for a white memory years ago put under frozen / for as it was then as it was now / for I sent him at last a postcard of my hometown / for no reason / for him to know / for on both sides it looked undressed from afar / for I did not know what to write / for I had lost his words in the nixe of the years / for I thought, What if he had moved from that forlorn place / for what to say when all has been said / for foresight / for givenness.

A Beltane Prayer

Calton Hill

AJ Clay

The starkness of the bitter, wind-chilled spring was always a surprise to Fiona when she left her flat and returned to these streets: the same rough paving slabs on which she'd worn out countless childhood shoes, traipsing to school. A few years ago, the tower block had carried the joyful mixture of family meals and the sound of laughter, magnified to a multitude in the stairwell. Now, there was only the pungent combination of stale cigarettes and the persistent damp, its tendrils marking the dull concrete around it. Here was the threshold between night and day, watched over by politicians in their distant plywood towers. As Fiona left for her errands, she passed a harried office worker, tapping out a harsh staccato in her heels. The only constant, unchanging part of her home was the rough feel of the wall under Fiona's fingertips, the curve of the staircase up to the tenth floor. It was a regular, Brutalist kind of magic, the sort that the rarified air of the New Town couldn't touch with its elegant austerity.

Soot-stained, haphazard buildings crowded around Fiona when she finally reached the heart of the Old Town. Sometimes, it smelled like it was still a meat market, and it was best not to question what was running down the gutter in sullen streams beside her. As soon as the familiar chaos of the Grassmarket crept into her ears, she felt herself relax.

On that first honeymoon day in Edinburgh, when everything had felt a little brighter, she'd taken her husband to the outdoor market, excitedly pointing at all the ingredients she remembered from her parents' meals. The stall holder handed over a golden shard of ginger, the ragged edges hinting at the fire contained within. Fiona breathed in its earthy, almost wooden smell. Her mother would set the gnarled root on the kitchen worktop, and as she cut it open the room would be filled with that pungent fragrance, demanding the cook's full attention. There would always be a few pieces left over from the dinner pot for Fiona, though. A tentative nibble would cause a narrowing of the eyes, a tickle in the throat, and her siblings' mockery. Over the years, that piquancy became a comfort, a reminder of those dinners together, and its fleshy firmness a memory of her family's warm embrace.

Fiona left the market laden with bags of spices, and found herself turning upwards towards the throngs on the Royal Mile. A woman bumped into Fiona with her pram; she gave an involuntary flinch when she saw it, but shook away the memory and walked on. Among the tourist tat shops, she found the small jewellers where she had bought the luckenbooth charm. Two hearts were still intertwined in the shop window, the silver gleaming in the fading light. For a moment she stood there, oblivious to the open-mouthed shoals of tourists flowing around her, and watched an old lady rearrange the display around the charm. Fiona's hands found their way to her neck, and she traced a finger around the outline of the hearts. Its magic hadn't been enough. She'd held his hand all that night ten years ago, and he'd given her the luckenbooth when he drew his last breath.

A salty tang from the Forth tinged the air when Fiona returned home and began the climb to her flat. A dozen storeys made the bags of shopping seem as heavy as her memories. The kitchen was her favourite room, because she could watch the volcano sleeping while she cooked, imagining the steamed windows were the result of its furious eruption, or the breath of the creatures that she knew dwelled beneath it.

Fiona thought it was perfect witchcraft, the way Arthur's Seat lay in the middle of the city, often mist-clad, watching over the quiet contest between Old and New Town. The fight was there in every street. She knew about the other battles that most people couldn't see; it was both a power and a burden her family had had to bear through the centuries.

When the mixture was cooked, Fiona opened the window and leaned out, letting the evening wind blow her long grey hair back. Soon it would be time to leave again. The bright yellow flames of gorse hanging over the doorway shed some of their petals as she brushed past them. She still kept the dried wedding bouquet, dotted with faded flowers from the wild bushes around town, in a box next to the empty, pristine cot.

The volcano's shadow crept along the grass of Holyrood Park, following Fiona as she approached the sheltered spot where the ceremony would take place. It was a custom she had observed every year since her husband had died, far from the rest of the crowds on Calton Hill drinking away the last hours before summer brought a bright renewal to the city.

A pall of smoke hung over the distant Beltane celebrations, dwarfing the bonfire Fiona had lit in a ring of stones before her. Inside her satchel, she'd brought more bunches of yellow flowers, a flask of pungent gingery broth, and an oatmeal bannock. On her way out, she'd run into the kindly old gentleman who lived next door; he had laughed and said 'it's a wee bit cold for a picnic at your age'. Still, he took the spare oatcake gratefully, not realising the power in her offering.

The fire crackled, sparks leaping upwards to join the stars. Fiona opened the flask and poured half of the broth onto the dark earth, an offering to the fairy folk living in the mound there. A bush rustled nearby and she stopped, turning round. Nobody had discovered her small rituals yet; most of the people she passed in the street were too ground down by their own worries to even notice the city around them. A rabbit scurried from the undergrowth and Fiona let out the breath she was holding, a cloud of mist gathering around her face.

She laid out her patchwork coat on the grass and sat down, watching the fire die down. Years of the same routine, and years of the same wait, alone in a city of thousands. Fiona looked up at the stars, more visible now that she was further from the orange glow of streetlights. *Wheels must turn as the seasons show, what lies dead shall surely grow.* That was the prayer being offered by the revellers gathered on the hill, their faces painted bright spring colours.

Eyes closed, Fiona felt the air turn warmer. He was late again. The grass rustled, as if someone was sitting down next to her. She opened her eyes and saw his broad shoulders, thick red beard and smiling eyes. Before Fiona could say anything, a familiar voice drifted to her ears.

'It's not long now. You'll see me soon.'

She closed her eyes again and smiled.

Meeting Places

Nicholson Square

Anne Ballard

It's a cruel wind today and the drizzle
stings sharp as hail, birls the large headscarves
of bundled-up Lebanese ladies
too cold to stop for a blether.

The Methodist Church has retreated,
neo-classic facade behind railings
bannered for Fair Trade Café, World Shop,
alternative therapies (in Hope's Garden)

while the nearby Mosque states its presence
by *Mosque Kitchen and Café* with car park,
Islamic Relief clothing banks, takeaway: *Tasty Curry
in a Hurry* – the Square's gesture to poetry.

A commotion of pigeons
in hopeful search of scraps from the slitter
of left-over lunches, take flight, protesting
in a crepitation of wings.

It's all a bit dreich, though enlivened
By *Palmyra Pizza, Lian Pu* Hot Pot and
Barbecue, *Elephants and Bagels*, and the inviting
Kurdish restaurant (BYOB).

In the garden the Tubal Cain column,
gifted to Edinburgh in 1909
by the East of Scotland Brassfounders,
stands to attention amid straggling daffs;
but the pretty fountain's agley, its flower petals
won't glisten with water again.

Witness

The Bridges

Nancy Somerville

It's one of those balmy evenings
when it seems it'll never get dark.

An old guy's collapsed in the bus shelter,
head in a pool of vomit
under the red plastic bench.
I've seen him before,
necking drink from a bottle.
A man in a green T-shirt takes his pulse,
a student doctor it transpires,
speaks numbers into his phone
as everyone else just stares.
I flag down the flashing lights,
direct the medics to where he lies
and they take over

but I'm restless, pumped with adrenaline,
walk to the next stop
where a young man sits on the kerb,
past caring
that cars are swerving to avoid his legs
and across the road another drunk
picks up a discarded supper,
gazes into the paper
then throws it at the gutter.

Above, swifts weave themselves
into the clear blue sky.

Freedom's Zone

Word Power Books

Bashabi Fraser

Now while the right and far right
Send seismic shocks through market place
And cultural hubs –

Now while nations within nations
Are silenced by fear and reprisals
Of mindless fury

We can walk into freedom's zone here
In this haven of wordsmiths
Who debate and denounce

Every low dishonest decade. Here is the
Beating heart of Scottish political thought
Flagged off by Kelman

Here the small press, the untold story
The hesitant pen – can all jostle in
and find a space to breathe

And bask beneath the delighted gaze
Of avid browsers gleaning the shelves
To claim the power of words.

On the Square

St Andrew Square

Jock Stein

Tangled rod ends dangle in their metal webs,
no longer able to conceal their reinforcement
of the hard core guts of money making
in this once rich square. High cranes take days
to launder work space, disengage blue cladding,
grab at rubbish concrete with their jagged jaws,
worrying it like a dog, dropping it in clouds
of dust controlled by well-aimed water sprays.

Such rough treatment of two million hours
of history... on his column, Viscount Melville
notices and gives an angry cough: first trams,
and now a shopping mall, what next, a helipad?
Is this the distant fruit of that enlightened brilliance
which propelled us to pan-European heights?
Or is it more the slow unpicking of Establishment,
so should we click at once on 'like', or be heart-sad?

The Square began with Dundas House, which soon became
the Royal Bank head office, with its hall and features
starring in some banknotes still in circulation.
The British Linen Bank was built upon its flanks
in 1806, and taken over by the Bank of Scotland.
The Union bank (now RBS) then gobbled up
the National Bank; with a sense of *dèjà vu* we ask,
'They regulate their clients... who regulates the banks?'

The famous lived there in the Square – Lord Henry
Brougham and David Hume, who hosted intellectual

dinner parties, probably without miraculous content.
He could not see arrive at number five a later
theist neighbour, National Bible Society, spreading
scriptures as the great philosopher once exported
his ideas. Today, instead of books and sparkling wine
and conversation, yawns a flat and empty crater.

Scottish Provident sold their Life Assurance first
in 1837. Their actuaries ruled like kings, and
one chipped daily golf balls from his office window
perfectly onto the grassy centre, till his status
changed from mild celebrity to minor criminal.
Spot on the Millennium, Abbey bought them over,
asset stripped them, took the loot to Glasgow
dodging history's question: 'Just how will they rate us?'

And where is old St Andrew in this pilgrimage of fame?
How does he match young Vincent Street and Charlotte Square,
with his chosen site gazumped by Melville's mansion?
Seems like money talks, and sainthood walks a furlong
further west to build a modest church in George Street.
On the demolition site, some railings shape a cross
held up on listed buildings pleading for survival,
while the Planners hold the key to right and wrong.

Dundas was 'on the square': at least he got the name
'Grand Manager of Scotland', or 'Ninth King Harry'.
Now labels cover all: this is a project shared
with Peveril Securities, though under Standard Life,
to turn the corridors of high finance into the lanes
between deodorant and toothpaste, with a nod
to history above – some office space, and at the top
the penthouse flats. Here is no sub-standard life.

The Guinea Pig at The Fruitmarket Gallery

The Fruitmarket Gallery

Rob A MacKenzie

(during Phyllida Barlow's 'Set' exhibition, summer 2015)

Tottering piles of planks! Paint-splattered cardboard
at improbable angles! The guinea pig has never known
such static contingency, such resistance to collapse
among the already collapsed. It owes its life to fear
of sudden movement, intricate shifts, cul-de-sacs.
It complains of an irresponsible lack of balance
between boulders, between choices. The guinea pig
has significant doubts over risk-free concepts of
stability. One twitch of a nose and a galaxy somewhere
sparks into quarks. It scents danger over light years of
darkness. In the gallery café, Imogen froths flat white
artworks; Ed's beard, symbol of bacchanalian glamour,
stirs to independent life. Iain cements his reputation
as a magnet for beautiful women. If things appear on
the slide, they hold true at root. If Edinburgh drinks
itself upright, the guinea pig will nudge it slantwise.
No matter how quietly it sits within the red tarpaulin
bodybag, the city will never feel quite quiet enough.

Pointless Comparison

Hebrides Bar

Sophie Scrivener

(for J.A.)

In Hebrides pub I wait for an afternoon train;
the bar stool is punishing, the whisky too weak.
Men butt heads and bray in amusement,
their wives and lovers reel in a state of excited
fermentation.

The barmaid sways, but stiffly,
her hips asynchronous to the beat.
She seems restless; her edges blurred
like the print in a soggy dictionary.

Her hoops of gold through soft lobes
rest on starched woollen shoulders,
and her hair is a bun of serpentine coils,
ends crisp with this morning's routine vanity
and this afternoon's spirit-soaked finger tips.

She is Jenny from the block
but a Cypriot.
She is not the woman I desire
but makes me long for the woman I do.

I write with shoulders hunched
and bow so close to the page,
I am half hoping to taste her
from between these lines.

a wish to lodge
New Waverley Development

Iain Morrison

Johnny come lately, come snooping,
the enclosing parapet is already consented.
Snap, from open view to framed view
including provision for people
with disabilities
But I, Johnny, have my own
Placemaking aims
Join me to see the north edge
of public viewing terrace pushed 0.5m
to the north. What the Old Town needs is
glazed link bridges
You receive the first
deficiency letter. Many follow,
'I would very much like for studio space
somewhere on the Royal Mile'
from aggrieved parties sensitive to
massing and architecture
'I lodge an objection in the strongest
possible terms.' The applicant has decided,
'A particular relief!', to withdraw
their application
for it   **uses too much glass,**
another of their tricks with light.
Daylighting, privacy and sunlight,
are three lensed entities scoping.
This window is not a good neighbour.
I am disturbed by the ever increasing no.
Reject this scheme in order to negotiate!
Edinburgh did not earn its world
heritage status for having lots of glass-

fronted buildings, where the floor
is held back from the facade
to allow the proportions of the arches
to read strongly. No it did not.
Are there any compelling reasons
that   **the "public" square will in fact be private**, why
we build houses on green space and
commercial white elephants on brown?

Sometimes I want to queen it
'the consent is not issued, sadly no it is not'
but it feels capricious of my offices
                to See past the tricks of their lightening
which is solely the responsibility of the sun.
Glitter of individuals sticks together
shouting into a tube
lots like trumpeting the wrong way round 'Good
practice to ensure contemporary artworks
                match the quality of the past' –
A little listening occurs to catch
signals attenuated appropriately
at the blowing end.
One thought once to turn the trumpet.
'Perhaps   **this proposal can also be delivered in isolation'**
Surely no it is not a half turn the residents desire
leading to chaotic chewing of plans over
a shiny brass daylighting.
Regroup and divide constantly, mes braves.
Interbreed too for a slower pulse.
Bicycle on   **a dynamic object perching between**
your legs. Your opportunities for wayfinding, new laid
take them newly. The woman photographing
on the footway is in fact only
a cypherwoman in an architect's preconstruction
framing the view.

The City and the City

The Scott Monument

Andrew Blair

Should we not
All
Be writing fantasies
Be
Our monuments digital
Or
Barriers

Should we not
Dwell
'neath a spire's subtle memes
Dreaming
Of the unique,
Novel

An artist's hedonism
Paradoxically demands
We traverse this city of literature
As biped drones homing dispassionate
The extraordinary everyday
Paving ways for abundance, avoidance
Revealed mid-autopsy of the chill:
Pipers' red hot branding
Registers chiming into subconscious pearls
Rage against Auld Reekie
As theme park,
The hero this city needs for hate
Is easier than wonder

Should we not
Note
The written word's silent edifice
So
Patient amid the bustle and
Flow

Should we not
Bask
Sharklike, misunderstood
Hemmed
In the greatest
Of shadows

sorry for our appearance
Princes Street

nick-e melville

flower bomb
the land of summer
in association with glamour
perversion mascara

make your make up last all day
conditions of the people
work your way
ask for your free sample

Scotland wears it best
they're real   honest
invented by bare minerals
indulge yourself for less

fresh new tea freshly picked
for quality cup
the new lipstick
from this bus stop

We are open
up to top man
down to top shop
sun glowing skin in a drop

a suit doesn't make the man
but it makes the man look great
visit the suite for more information
cedar wood state

nurse clinic in-store
personalised moisturising routine
lingerie second floor
ask us about your perfect protein

excuse us while we change
the secret heart collection
sorry for our appearance
please ring for attention

awaken eyes
smooth lines
pinch me!
76% agree

An Xmas Exit

The Christmas Market

Martin McIntyre

There's not even enough festive illumination left
to bounce off the high-viz jackets of the
strike-it-all-down staff
at 4.20; black and dreich
might never ask:
that Polish waffle-lady,
the Romanian candle-waxer,
the Slavic bratwurster,
the well-hung Scottish bunner-boy
if dreich also exists drearily in German
or is it only that it should
by sound,
independent of Berlin's Marlene Dei-
who once was Mary Magdalene.

Actually, there are still a few
anaemic bulbs blinking across
the spokes of the seized big-wheel
now de-nuded of its rocking-chairs
dead of all anticipatory screams, dismembered.

Get they pallets aff ma base will ye!
a tired, de-bronzed, Adam Black insists,
Adieu or bloody go! A man for letters I wis: naebody's fey funny fool

Little wonder Santa bailed out
over a week ago: tinsel-tortured,
scunnered with consumption on a grand-scale,
the sequelae.

Nor is it such a straightforward gig for the round guy these
    days
- mild, exhausting, weather in all the gear
- a melange of multi-cultural needs to meet
- technology that outstrips and outplays
reindeer sweat, thumbs down
not to mention the increasing pressure to double-
up as Jesus: stille nacht, heilige nacht an' all that.

Anyway, until whenever – Happy New Years to all and sundry.

Indifferent Snails

Heart of Midlothian

Tessa Berring

Indifferent snails
creep across scaffolds
in the same way
the present
creeps around the past
with immeasurable gobs
of spit.

Marble Table

National Gallery of Scotland

Lauren Pope

So close to the centre
of attention.
Sweaty-palmed visitors
knead your face
as they lean in to see
'Diana and Actaeon' –
the masterpiece.

But Titian himself
would have admired you,
lingered over your Jupiter swirls,
wrestled to equal them with his palette
of Carmine Lake and Orpiment,
recognised your birthplace, Siena,
as just down the road from his;

your classical ancestry,
his predecessors' medium of choice –
your ability to mimic the softness of skin
or the glow of a youthful face;
the way delicacy trickles from strength,
time just another word for *chisel*.

Free Fall

Edinburgh Waverley

Jane Griffiths

Last night I dreamed I went to Waverley again –
there were the ascending girders and engine
noise, the descending cabs with their human
traffic, and between them the walkways' slick
drip-dripping internal rain.
                              And that man –
the unknown one whose death we read about,
months ago, who leaped from North Bridge
in full possession of his single-minded self
and his body filling its contours to perfection
cleanly as if the loch could still receive him –
                              he was busking
over by Smiths at the bottom of the concourse
and inaudible in its echo-chamber of calling points.

Above the starred glass canopy shadowed flags
and birds lifted a beat too slow. Listen, he said,
there are places we don't go. Last night I dreamed
my song, wind-dubbed, flying upwards. Listen,
he said, last night I dreamed the words for it:
they were not this fiction. They were present
continuous, and real as stone or water. Like this,
he said. Listen. I'll take it from the top, again.

Waverley Song

Edinburgh Waverley

Dominic Hale

There is no better antidote against entertaining too high an opinion of others, than having an excellent one of ourselves at the very same time. – W.S.

But when ye come back oot ay Waverley Station eftir being away fir a bit, ye think: Hi, this isnae bad. – I.W.

O utter singing shit! the transpennine cancelled
   mid-comedown from a handsome event
shirking edinburgh university's privately
   educated & aesthetic coterie
necessarily remarkable & assessing the recent
   city breaks & various
institutions of sunless capital cities

   i daydreamt about burning media proprietors
w/ cigarettes booting that tory in the
   shin in the multinational era
fat globe shifting & eating whole rigid
   woods of fauna itching outside wh
smith to simulate a budget revolution or not
   applying for prestigious literary scams

trains are fleeting thru my skull might od
   paracetamol for a huge autumn joke acknowledge
our complicity & jump off the north
   bridge w/ bland herring gulls
language being insatiable of course the
   sickliness of the allocated earth of screens
sharing this deficient crush of life & ownership

Waverley

Edinburgh Waverley

Iain Matheson

You'll have a favourite book
of verse in your overcoat,
its cover will be yellow.

Your pullover will be stained,
very likely gravy from
the savoury chicken pie

you were served by that surly
girl with her gravestone tattoo,
with her badge which said Shirley.

It will be Wednesday; at
such an early hour no-one
will have come to wave goodbye.

The Castle

Edinburgh Castle

Sophie Cooke

Myned Agned: winged rock. Here's
the place from which we breathe. Solid,
airborne.
Its walls are accordion ribs – in, out,
go all the fighting men, and fleeing folk
from farms aroundabout.

In, out. How can you count the breaths
you've taken, in your life?
So normal are its battering and sieges,
backing down and setting out.

But then
this is the place that takes down its own defence
so its strength cannot be taken, used against
the folk it is set on protecting.
Rock by rock and stone by stone the Bruce undid it –

'til only a wee chapel stood on the windy clifftops.
You can keep your soft heart, up there,
with no fear it will be misused.

Stewart kings built later walls and towers,
put up new cannon. But we remember
the time of stripping down – of no more soldiers,
no jewelled crowns, and how
the walls up there still made a place to breathe from.

It is a bright fire in dark times: bastion.
Din Eidyn, Eden's fortress,
the Castle in the Gardens.

The Mound Before Midnight

Playfair Steps

Janette Ayachi

the sun.

The one o'clock gun sets a cluster
    of brazen city birds into hasty flight,
        a fiddler on the Playfair steps serenades
            the crowds with his medieval glissando
                pouring rhythm into their march towards

Museum Trip

National Museum of Scotland

Marianne MacRae

Why are these masks so small?
They look hungry. Don't you think
they look thin and hungry?
I can almost see their vocal cords
singing for their supper.

The sound and vision section
is everybody's favourite
because in here we can bury
our grieving in the cheerful gong
and clatter of interactive displays.

Dinosaur bones are boring because
they look like solid dust.
In dreams I have hung from the tip
of a Tyrannosaurus rib and from there
I saw mountainsides burning.

These girls have nice faces.
I feel like they might haunt me at night time.
Everything in the olden days
(including the women)
was decorated with hair, fur or feathers.

I like it because it is old.
I like it because of the clothes.
I like it because in the still, almost-warmth
of the do-not-touch deer hides
I feel like we are not alone.

Valhalla

Calton Hill

Ricky Monahan Brown

I've borrowed a book of Edinburgh city walks from the library, to get my bearings back. This one takes me through the Old Calton Burial Ground, which Abraham Lincoln benevolently surveys from a plinth. His monument marks the graves of five Scots who died in the Civil War, all on the Union side.

Uncertain of the details of my journey after a long absence, I've been repeatedly taking my phone out of my pocket to check my progress. Edinburgh always claimed to be on seven hills, like Rome, its spiritual predecessor. Arthur's Seat, Blackford Hill, Braid Hills, Castle Hill, Corstorphine Hill, Craiglockhart Hill, and the one I'm on now. Or maybe it's the seven in the old rhyme:

> *Abbey, Calton, Castle grand,*
> *Southward see St Leonard's stand,*
> *St John's and Sciennes as two are*
> *given, And Multrees makes seven.*

Or maybe the map in my pocket is right, and Edinburgh is really built on countless hills and under innumerable bridges, a labyrinthine rat run. But the Nelson Monument looms above, so I take a chance on my gut and head up a narrow, stone, tree-lined set of stairs signposted as "Jacob's Ladder". Because going with my gut always worked before, I wryly reflect.

Re-emerging into the light, I orient myself again. Horatio's 105-foot telescope still stands on its end to the north, but a little closer now. Peering deep into Edinburgh's heart. So I cross Calton Road and set off up another flight of stone steps to the summit. Halfway up, a monk in grey robes and Reeboks stops me with an expectant smile. He passes me a little plastic amulet bearing an exhortation to *WORK SMOOTHLY* for *LIFETIME PEACE*, and opens a small flip book to a picture of his temple. Then he passes me another little booklet and a pen, indicating that I can fill in my name, home country, a message of peace, and a pledge. I fish in the pocket of my jeans for a pound coin, and the monk thanks me with another smile.

He indicates the little yellow flowers crowding into the stairway and tells me in quiet, halting English, 'When the gorse is in bloom, it is the kissing time.'

I smile back and nod.

When I reach the top of the hill, I smell the salty sea air blowing across the flat, open expanse of the park. I mark a cross on Calton Hill, and stuff the map back into my pocket. Above, a plane slices a contrail across the blue sky, having turned the shoulder of North Berwick.

That was always my favourite part of the flight back from New York, seeing the harbours of Leith and Edinburgh laid out 5,000 feet below. Like the map I once poured across my parents' living room floor, tracing from where Mum fished me out of Newhaven harbour at low tide to where Paw watched as I righted myself after capsizing under the Forth Rail Bridge. But I never took that flight often enough. Not even after the desks at Cantor Fitzgerald, eighty floors above the desk of my late wife, were turned to dust. Dust that silted up the Hudson River, the Diamond Reef, and the lungs of New York City's rescue workers.

Having taken a few breaths of recollection, I start towards the top of the monument. Just a few steps into the 143 whitewashed stairs spiralling upward, the frame of a recessed window relays the message, *Almost there.*

'How brilliantly Edinburgh!' I think. It's still inside me, twenty years later. Even now, when Chloë flies away to visit her parents in South Carolina, I can feel the petrifying stoicism spreading outwards again to cold fingers and toes.

Closer to the top of the tower, another message in neat black paint exhorts me to *Keep going on!* And I do. All the way to the thin door in time-travelling blue that, if two strangers push and pull it together, can be opened out onto a spectacular view over the National Monument, towards the Kingdom of Fife. The ships in the Forth contrast with the boats of the new Scottish Parliament lying keels-upward in the shadow of the tower, wishing their architect's Mediterranean sun could dry them out. The ships in the firth are alive and productive, like the fishing boats my grandfather's friends sailed. I think of him taking me to see Jimmy, who would lie on his waterbed in Seafield Hospital changing the channels on the television by blowing into an air pipe. The fisherman had broken his neck falling through an open hatch in the deck of his boat. The waterbed was to prevent bedsores, but Jimmy would let a fascinated wee boy up on it, too. Of course, I didn't see the tragedy. Only the excitement of the new, and the generous, garrulous fisherman. But now, the boats just remind me that Hugh and Jimmy are gone, and my mother, too. Back in Auld Reekie with my tail between my legs, taking this walk for the first time in too long, it will take time for this to become a new version of home.

I bring my view back down to Edinburgh's Folly, the landmark I've really come to see. Since moving back, I've been walking around the city and re-learning its rhythms and routes. With Chloë in tow, I find myself taking unexpected, meandering detours that unveil new views, as well as more obvious, expository routes. Walking east along Princes Street, the gothic rocket ship of the Scott Monument hadn't looked as tall as it did back in the day. But it has a heft I don't remember. From there, Scotland's National Monument looked like it should be all the way down in Leith. Like its spiritual successor, the tram, it only gets as far as the East End.

Scanning the folly from my telescopic aerie, I try to map for myself how the balance of Playfair and Cockerell's plans for the monument might have lain. Particularly the catacombs that were intended, two hundred years ago, to form *Scotland's Valhalla*, a place where the nation's heroes would have been put to rest. A place where Jimmy and my grandfather might have been comfortable, after those wartime special operations in Albania and Malaysia. Not somewhere for a Scot who should have died three thousand miles away after a day spent eating fancy pizza, drinking, smoking, and shagging.

But I can't build the chambers from absence, so I tumble back down the narrow stairs of the tower to have a look from ground level. Down here, the monument's few pillars are overwhelming, and I'm aware that it has acquired a power to move as a palimpsest that it could never have had in its complete state.

A caravan of Spanish tourists in bright anoraks is rolling down towards the road. As their laughter blows over Holyrood Park towards Duddingston Loch, it seems I've been left with the place to myself. I sit on a low rock and root myself down into the land. Eyes closed, I'm imagining the grass spreading over my boots and pulling me in. When I open my eyes again, I'm surprised to see a wee boy sitting atop the monumental steps. I walk over, and with effort haul myself up to join him.

He doesn't look like one of the Spaniards, this blond, ruddy-cheeked laddie.

'Hullo.' His speech confirms it.

'Hello to you, wee man. How did you manage to get up here? I'm fair puggled.'

'The same way as you.'

That settles it, I suppose. The slightness of his frame must have compensated for those wiry little arms and legs.

'I like your cardie,' I tell him.

'Thanks. My mammy knitted it for me.'

We sit in silence for a moment, then he reaches into his pocket for a plastic toy. He presses a button to extend it into full operational mode, and waves it up and down my side. I squint.

'Don't worry,' the boy reassures me. 'The sonic screwdriver indicates that all your circatrigintan rhythms are normal.'

'That's a relief,' I tell the prodigy. 'But what's a circatrigintan rhythm when it's at home?'

He giggles and confesses he has no idea. It's a word he's heard his mother use.

'That's okay. Can I have a look at that?'

Appreciating the interest, the lad hands over the toy. I replicate his motions.

'Oh! Two hearts!' I exclaim. 'Are you Doctor Who?'

'No, but I am a Time Lord,' the lad explains with great emphasis, as if to a smaller child.

'Oh, good! I've been wanting to ask someone – I was watching a science programme, and they said that time travel is possible, but only backwards. Is that right?'

'Oh, no!' he tells me. 'I can travel to the future, too. How else could I get back if I visited the past?'

I explain to him that I managed to travel to New York in the 1990s.

'Really? How did you get back here?' the Time Lord asks.

'I had to take the long way back.'

That seems to satisfy him. The lad and I sit for a while, quiet, save for the muted thump of his trainers swinging against the stone steps. After a few minutes, I see Chloë heading along the path towards us, the Doric columns behind me and the boy scattering sunlight around her. Bang on time.

I turn back to him.

'Look, I know you're a Time Lord and all, but is your mum around?'

'Oh yes. She's down over the other side.'

'Good,' I reply, craning round to face where the catacombs would have been. I see the head of a woman giving her wee man just enough space to start exploring the world for himself.

'Robbie!' she calls. 'Leave the man alone. It's time to go home!'

'Is that your mum?' I stage whisper, conspiratorially.

The boy nods. Before he goes, I want to tell him that traveling backwards in time is really difficult, too. That if you don't get things right the first time, it's hard to go back and fix them. And if you find yourself holed up in hospital after being shot in a botched mugging in the West Village, you might not get to say all the things you want to say before your mum leaves.

But he doesn't need to know that yet. It's so beautiful up here today.

'OK. Look, before you go... I was bluffing when I said I didn't know much about time travel. I need you to take a message to your mum.

'You run over, and tell her that you met a traveller from the future, and that he told you that you're gonna do just fine. Alright?

'Good.'

Heaven and Earth

St. Giles' Cathedral

Emma Sedlak

Returning is an awkward motion.
It has been months, and
these stones are not as we left them.
   The morning service sermons
   love has come among us like a child.
You make me feel like a child.
Words are put into my mouth
and swallowed like bread and wine.
   Holy, holy, holy,
     the ghosts are hungry.
A strained connection,
some feigned relationship.
But I'm lonely in your company.
   Heaven and earth
   are full of your silences.
I appear lost now.
Does that make it
easier to let me go?
   The sea has prepared the dry land
   and has made hardened hearts to kneel.
I was grieved
with the known temptations
   of the wilderness,
  and said
in the beginning we saw
a world without end.

Gardyloo

Mary King's Close

Miriam Gamble

(To Andrew Chesney, the last inhabitant of Mary King's Close)

Shit surfaced outside our flat last week
– Easter holidays, what's to be done? –
and I thought of you, proud
on your modern indoor throne,
the door flung open so that all could see you.
Shit scrolling down the street to the Nor' Loch
at seven and, *le soir*, at ten. On iced shit,
treacherously, people slipping forwards.

Forwards to the future, to me
with the toe of my boot going *What is that?*
AH JESUS!! mincing down the road
like my whole self's coated in miasmas,
my partner begging *Would you drop it?*
Ten o'clock on a Friday night and shit
on the public pavement by our window.
Andrex bloomed from the exploded drain like stars,

like subterranean flowers or the delicate
caparison of folks long sealed and stoppered,
douked into a rancid skin it took ten
minutes for your head to sink beneath,
all property repurposed by the town.
Hanging for men; for women a sick,
slow sputter in the pleasure gardens,
the guide's pun withering: *A crappy way to go*.

At the eye of the compulsory purchase shit
storm you, adamant but beaten, the street's
noise silenced and your gem, your dunny,
abandoned to the arsenic-covered walls.
Well, fine, I hear you say, and at ten o'clock,
with the St Giles tipping order, you cast
this tickertape, these shredded documents, this --
on the Athens of the North's sumptuous grey.

The Statue of David Hume

The Royal Mile

Ruth Aylett

Davie, what's with the toga?
What happened to your bonny
red and gold jackets,
embroidered waistcoats?
Just up from St Giles too;
some kind of a joke
though it's not so clear
whether on them or on you.

Not dressed for dreich days
with one shoulder bare;
tablet propped on your knee
to show you could read?
Seems the sculptor disliked you
thought it droll to portray
you shoeless for the superstitious
to touch-polish your toe.

So you were right Davie,
it's mostly passion not reason
when we choose what to do,
and right again that we know
what smacks into our senses,
as this statue does for sure.
A counterfeit "wisdom"
with classical pretentions.

Redrawing The Lines

St. Giles' Cathedral

Keith Dumble

It's the oldest one I could find.

Paper so thin it's more a memory than a map. Still recognisable though. Still fit for purpose. The Castle, a black fist atop broken bones of rock. Arthur's Seat a declawed lion, dreaming of its youth, of when it gouged the land into this blanket wrinkle of hills. Around the city, a wall, long since smashed by Edinburgh's unruly spurts of growth. Inside its protective boundary, individual houses stand confident side-by-side, safety in numbers.

Perfect.

I concentrate. Focus my temporal lobe until the lines float up from the parchment, a ghost city shimmering above my desk. I wait until the mistplane is fully-formed, the summit of Arthur's Seat the last thing to solidify.

I sever my cord, swoop down. Down through the grim clouds of reality, down until the feet of my soul touch straw-strewn streets. I gag against the meat-turned stench, so strong it bites at my inner cortex.

I take a moment to acclimatise, to avoid the swamping rush of overload. The voices I hear sound foreign; single, simple words are all I catch. I hear one – *kirk* – and grasp at it, clinging to its familiarity. Use it to pull myself in, deeper. Until I can bear to open my eyes.

The church stabs at heaven. It's older – and newer – than the one I know. Without its crowned spire, the refined architecture of the steeple appears to have mistaken the midden-muddle of Edinburgh for the more ordered streets of Rome or Florence. It disorients me for a moment; I think I've miscalculated. But no, it *is* St Giles'.

I pull out for a moment, study the map. The hand-drawn cross on top of the church points to a line between two houses on the other side of the High Street. I spin a coin in my head, wait for it to stop. Tails it is. I choose the house on the left, the one with more markings. I drag myself back through the mistplane, back to the streets, back in front of the cathedral.

The object sits heavy in my pocket, each tick of its hands is a moment passing unmarked into history. I take it out, check it's still in one piece. The glass is solid, the intricate workings of the sphere inside throb with a mechanical heartbeat.

I cross the road, passing through a horse dragging a cart piled high with manure. The animal senses me, whinnying. The driver does not; he whips the beast and curses it using sharp-edged words I'm glad I don't understand.

The house I've chosen looms up like a cliff, with glassless windows like hermits' caves. The door hangs on one hinge; a smear-faced child lolls on the doorstep, playing with a piece of wood carved into the splintered likeness of a person. I step past, into the darkness. The smell is overpowering; I put my hand over my mouth and nose but it sears inside, threatening to drag out the contents of my stomach.

I feel the echo ache of my severed cord, the silent scream of my cortex. I'm forced to work quick. I find a place, a cellar of sorts. Rats glare as I scrape a patch of dirt with my heel. The ground's soft, more mud than earth. I dig down, create a hole, deep enough. I place the device inside, cover it with the clogging clay then press down with my feet, trampling straw into the surface. Concealed.

The air outside brings little relief. The sky is a glower. Exploratory drops of rain parachute down, spotting the street. I walk back to the cathedral. Its bells are ringing, calling the faithful.

I close my eyes. Vision my way back. I rise, floating above the city. Its lines blur, ghosting back through time. I'm bird-high above it now. Lines crumble, fall. Fade back into the parchment. I grab my cord, reattach it to my present self. Breathe.

I fold the map carefully, putting it in the box. I lock the lid and place it in the hollow beneath the false floorboard.

It should be safe there.

It has to be.

*

'You found it?' The sharp-faced man shoots doubt at me, like I'm a cheap parlour magician who's just pulled a dead rabbit from a hat.

'Of course.' I reach into my jacket, bring out the object. 'Just as you asked.'

'How...?' He shakes his head, slipping the once-lost thing into his pocket. 'No matter. Cartomancers. You're all the same.'

'Meaning?' I raise a smile. The insults bounce off me.

'Secretive. Like closed books.'

'Closed atlases, perhaps.'

He ignores my attempt at humour, sliding an envelope across the desk. It's not as fat as I'd hoped. 'This is what we agreed.'

I don't insult either of us by looking inside. I rise, offering my hand. 'A pleasure doing business with you.'

'I appreciate your discretion.'

'Your secrets are safe with me.' As if his secrets mattered.

'Goodbye.'

I know I'll never see him again. I never have repeat customers.

I fold up the map of Hong Kong, file it in its correct chronological position on my shelves. I may go back there for pleasure some day, I catch myself thinking, before I remember.

I check my diary. Blank paper floods the rest of the day. A meeting with a colleague this evening, in sixteenth-century Florence.

I try not to look at the entry for tomorrow, but it looms dark on the page, the shadow of an executioner's axe.

Tomorrow. I will go back to Edinburgh.

To nineteen sixty-seven.

To activate the device.

★

We stroll through the pristine courtyard of the Uffizi, our shadows stretching out before us. The warmth of the sun does its best to lift my spirits. Merchants and bankers eye each other with secular mistrust, slaves to gods of gold and greed. Bells from nearby churches call the diminishing faithful to worship at another altar.

'You are sure?' My friend passes through a group of men arguing in allegro Florentine. 'It will be a one-way journey. No map to guide you back.'

I stare out towards the Arno, a thread of gold veined through the city's heart. 'It's the only way.'

'Why Edinburgh? Why not somewhere more dramatic? The Five Points of New York, or the revolutionary streets of Paris, perhaps.'

'It's personal.' I leave it at that.

'And you're sure four hundred years is long enough? For the device to have stored enough power?'

I think back to the cellar of the house on the High Street. To the machine, buried beneath straw and filth. Ticking its way through the centuries, counting down time until it's ready to fulfil its purpose.

'You doubt my calculations?'

'No, my friend. I question your motives.'

A group of barefoot children scuttle past, laughing and shouting. 'Believe me, I have explored every other possibility.'

'You plan to do it tomorrow?'

'At noon.' I imagine the bells of St Giles', sounding for the last time.

'Have you stopped to think what this might mean for the rest of us?'

'The maps are mockeries of the truth. Our order has become corrupted.'

'So you plan to destroy it?'

'I plan to put things right.'

'You will unravel a thread which cannot be repaired. The changes that they ... that *we* have made will be undone in an instant.'

'We had no right to make them in the first place. We should have left the past alone.'

'Some good has come of it, surely?'

'It was never our right.'

The children are gone. The courtyard is empty. 'Then whose right was it? God's?'

A flock of scrawny pigeons cloud from the roof of the palace, flying towards the darkening sky. I say nothing.

'Why tell me?' he asks. 'Aren't you afraid I will try to stop you?'

'I tell you so you have a chance to be as far from the Atlas as you can. I tell you because you are my friend.'

He looks up past the tower. 'You are certain of this?'

We rise, unfolding ourselves from the map. The streets of Florence become sketches once more, inked on centuries-old parchment.

'I am,' I say, feeling the rush of the present accelerate towards me through the mistplane. 'I have made up my mind.'

'So be it.' His voice is a trace. 'Goodbye, old friend.'

I wish him farewell, but we're already out.

★

I smooth out the map. Ordnance survey accurate. The city as it was, forty-eight years ago. Less cluttered, enough room to breathe. A city with a dream of its future.

I calibrate my cortex like a compass.

The lines rise. The ordered grid of the New Town, a refined matrix shimmering above my desk. The spinal column of the Royal Mile, its closes thin arteries threading down on either side. The crown of St Giles', rising above it all.

I'm in.

The smells are familiar, though the air tastes cleaner. The High Street is busy; the Festival is in full swing. Crowds jostle outside the cathedral, craning necks for the best view of a thin man in a dinner jacket performing magic tricks.

I look up. Twin contrails criss-cross the blue sky, creating a saltire. Tourists point up with boxy cameras. I take solace from it: a portent, a sign of forthcoming victory.

I cross the street, the cobbles worn beneath my shoes. The house has trebled in height since I was last here. It stands squeezed between its siblings, its ground floor given over to a shop which claims to sell only the finest Scottish goods.

I wonder, looking up at the sightless sockets of its windows, if the building remembers. If it has an awareness of its past, of its youth, when it slouched here with surly teenage confidence. I wonder if it had a premonition of what it would become, what its place on the map would be.

A cold wind. I feel them. The others.

They're coming.

I imagine them, paging through their copies of the Atlas, trying to locate me. My friend had been right: they would be expecting somewhere more dramatic, somewhere more intricately mapped.

But they've still found me. The echo of my cortex, pulsing like a pinprick dot on a radar. And now they raise the lines from their own copies of the same map, zooming into these same streets.

I don't have much time.

I enter the shop. Slip behind the counter, through the

dozing shopkeeper. Into the storeroom, the peat tang of whisky heady and thick.

A cellar door, metal. Locked. I close my eyes, sketch out a map of the room. The lines blue, like an architect's drawing. I alter them.

The hole gapes in the floor. Darkness.

I don't need light. I can sense the device, its energy. Still here, where I buried it yesterday, four hundred years ago. Where it has lain, charging. And now primed, ready.

Ready for the final map to be drawn.

I hear them. In the shop, above me. Their footsteps, hurried. Desperate.

I crouch down. The cellar floor is packed earth. I detect the device. Uncover it.

It pulses in my hands. The lines on the globe inside it glow. Another world.

A better world.

I open the device, separate the hemispheres of the globe with a seismic twist of my wrist. The core inside is a brilliant star, warm to the touch.

Voices above me. The lines of the cellar shift. I close my fingers around the shining heart of the world.

It was a good choice. Edinburgh. Here, now, in nineteen sixty-seven.

It was here, in this city. Where I met her. A long time ago.

A time which here, now, has yet to be born.

We'll never meet. She'll never be. Not as she was.

She'll never feel the pain.

I squeeze my fist. Feel the crack. It's more fragile than I expected.

I'm granted a final moment.

A glimpse of the new map of the world.

Vault

Edinburgh Vaults

Agnes Marton

I'm the ghost of the South Bridge
(perhaps a victim of Burke and Hare),
welcome to Most Haunted.
Let's walk through The Caves, The Rowantree,
and what was Adam Square,
kicking casks and jars
in deaf arches
of the damp.

Lick the stones.
They are savoury and loud,
almost iron.
Try to remove your lips.
Draw bisons with your tongue.

I crave soup but
all I eat is
brick stew with grass,
it stains my teeth.

I beat mud meringue
without cream,
adding all the dirt at once.

I wolf it down
like in tales
the beast would swallow
the milk-angered maid.

Now my smile stinks of sour greed,
it still bites into my guts.
Wish I could climb an enladdered scream,
wish I could taste ice
and blood and kiss and water.

Cheeky Burdies

The World's End Pub

Finola Scott

One for sorrow. Two for joy
It squats twa-faced oan thi corner,
midnicht blue as a magpie's wing,
lookin doon & roon thi brae
linkin Castle an Palace

wi Parliament richt at thi boddom.
Aince by thi gates in thi city wall
it teetered oan thi edge, ootside nowhere,
inside thi whale world – Edinburgh.

Fir thon pair o bricht lassies oot fir a nicht
oan thi toon it wis thi end o thi world.
Nae mair they'd dance tae David Cassidy,
nae mair sing wi thi Osmonds.

Three for a girl. Four for a boy. Five for young.

Noo tourists gang in thi dank pub
tae savour real Edinburgh,
tae scoff cullen skink, haun-tied leeks
an bowls o creamy crowdie.

Then it wisnae real ale or reid wine,
jist wee haulfs sooked in dark
corners by quiet men leanin
oan their elbows waitin fir time.

But ane o those men wisnae jist quiet.
He eyed them wi derk thouchts, laffed,
lured then bound them, leavin them,
thi judge telt, like carrion fir aw tae see.

Six for old. Seven for a secret never to be told

John Knox Returns
John Knox House

Christine De Luca

Nae doot hit dusna budder dee, but hit's
a peety dat da graveyard o da High Kirk
 – whaar famously du preached –
is jöst a car park; an, laek King Richard,
der nae richt steyn ta mark dy layer.

If du wis here daday, du'd be weel wint
wi what du caa'd da *Munstrous Regiment
o Weemen*. Heth! Der rinnin aathin noo:
da kirk, da country!   Du'd maybe shaa
da wye again in scölin bairns.   An I reckon

du'd reesel up ithin da Kirk; likkly stert
anidder Reformation, for theology can sturken.
Some still bigg nairrow chapels, coont angels
dancin apö da tap o preens an pick oot
passages o scripture ta suit der prejudice.

Du'd be rantin aboot refugees, seekin
wyes ta hoose da haemless, feed da fantin;
aksin da Rabbi an da Imam in for tae,
tweetin da Pope, dancin at da Méla an
haein a peerie hooch on Hogmanay.

An fae dy fine-laek hoose prunk i da Netherbow
du'd hail hen-pairties stotterin doon da Mile,
aa bare trams an tattoos; shooer a peerie blissin
whan dey'd blaa dee droothie smoorikins.
Dey'd tak a selfie wi dee if du lat dem.

John Knox Returns

John Knox House

Christine De Luca

No doubt it doesn't bother you, but it's
a pity that the cemetery of the High Church
 – where famously you preached –
is just a car park; and, like King Richard,
there's no headstone to mark your layer.

If you were here today, you'd be well acquainted
with what you called the *Monstrous Regiments
of Women*. Heavens! They're running it all now:
the church, the country! You'd maybe show
the way again in schooling children. And I reckon

you'd stir things up within the church, likely start
another Reformation, for theology can congeal.
Some still build narrow chapels, count angels
dancing on the heads of pins and pick out
passages of scripture that suit their prejudice.

You'd be ranting about refugees, seeking
ways to house the homeless, feed the hungry;
asking the Rabbi and the Imam in for tea,
tweeting the Pope, dancing at the Méla and
having a little knees-up on Hogmanay.

And from your handsome house in the Netherbow
you'd hail hen-parties falling about down the Mile
all bare limbs and tattoos; return a little blessing
when they'd blow you drunken kisses.
They'd take a selfie with you if you let them.

Sae step doon aff yun plint, man, come dee wys
an trim yun muckle baerd, change dy eemage.
I hear du laid in a barrel o da best Burgundy
for dy wake: can du spare a gless?
Hit's time ta share a tipple tae da future!

So step down off that plinth, man, come away
and trim that bushy beard, change your image.
I hear you laid in a barrel of the best Burgundy
for your funeral party: can you spare a glass?
It's time to share a tipple to the future!

Kunstkammer Corner

Museum of Edinburgh

Samuel Tongue

A poem is a *Kunstkammer*, a cabinet
of curiosities, a collection of monstrosities
thrown together and labelled to set
the mind a-flush with a city's possibilities.
But a poem is also full of fakes,
oojamaflooks and thingymebobs
like Mrs Rabbie Burns' green oatcakes;
the death masks of Burke and Hare, robbed
from their gurning faces; the fables
attached to the founding of HolyRood.
Or Robert Louis Stevenson's golf-ball
stitched with his initials (he would
forever slice his drive into the long grass).
Here's the silver whistle alleged
to have coaxed the first train across
the miracle of the Forth Rail Bridge.
Here's a photo of Field Marshal Haig
aged three, in a dress, with a pistol.
I can already see the vague
outline of those whiskers, the lists
of war-dead. John Knox's spectacles
are not in their case – he lost them chasing
Greyfriars Bobby down the optical
illusion of Tolbooth Wynd, racing
Adam Smith's weaving mother.
This, of course, is a lie, another
story, another open cabinet of a poem,
just like a *Kunstkammer* in a museum.

Childish Things

The Museum of Childhood

Tessa Berring

I
Childish Things

Had they given her a papier-mâchè bulldog
instead of plastic, non-absorbent foals;
and had she licked her egg cups clean,
slung china dolls over home-made cliffs,
she may have understood what life is.
She wouldn't be out there smeared in jelly,
searching for a god in the butcher's shop.

II
Transistor

That was the day her doll
swallowed the radio, tuned it
to screams in its pink
celluloid belly, till her soul
split open like an almond.

It was no surprise
she fled to the city,
to find a place
where no small helicopter
could ever, ever land.

III
Papier Mâché Bulldogs, France, 1910.

Dissolved paper bulldogs
look like '*puddles with no teeth*',
(he really wished the teeth
had survived).

But Loulou and Sebastien
have eyes like hardened egg yolks
and that is quite enough
for a nightmare.

At the Fringe

Royal Mile

Tracey S. Rosenberg

They're Edinburgh's greatest trial.
They dress in most outrageous styles.
They stalk you on the Royal Mile –
       They're actors at the Fringe.

You simply want to see some shows
and tour a haunted mouldy close
but they will never let you go.
       They're actors at the Fringe.

Just try to swerve away from him!
He'll block your path and raise a din:
"Fringe First! Five stars! 'The next Big Yin!'"
       He's acting at the Fringe.

You can't sweep her away with brooms.
Glance at a poster: there she looms!
She's on at the Assembly Rooms.
       She's acting at the Fringe.

They'll buttonhole you in a queue.
It doesn't matter which – Tattoo,
the Hub, the Castle, or the loo.
       They're actors at the Fringe.

The *List* has dubbed them "worst in show".
The Underbelly's banned them – so
has BBC at Potterow.
       They're actors at the Fringe.

She haunts the Famous Spiegeltent.
He busks and begs to pay his rent.
Their audience is heaven-sent!
       They're actors at the Fringe.

He wears a cloak, she wears a ruff.
On warm days they pose in the buff.
September can't come soon enough
       for actors at the Fringe.

He shouts! She bounces! They perspire!
Attention-seeking whinging liars –
No, I don't want your &$*$^$% flyer!
       Stop acting at the Fringe!

Enquiry Desk

Scottish Poetry Library

Andy Jackson

Do you have the one
with that poem they read at the funeral
in that movie?

Do you have the one
with that poem that they used to make us
learn at secondary school?

Do you have the one
with that poem that the Librarians decided was
too beautiful to catalogue and classify?

Do you have the one
with that poem that knows the difference between
ae thing and *anither thing*?

Do you have the one
with that poem that sat in the corner for ten years and then
exploded like a grenade in a crowded space?

Do you have the one
with that poem from the box of love letters
the city keeps under its bed?

Do you have the one
with that poem that identifies the chemical properties
of the ghosts of ideas it contains?

Do you have the one
with that poem that is a cache of weapons
which can never be put beyond use?

Do you have the one
with that poem that has learned to impersonate
other poems it has never met?

Do you have the one
with that poem that has mastered chiaroscuro
yet can also emulsion a room in an hour?

Do you have the one
with that poem that stole into my lover's bed
when I wasn't reading it?

Do you have the one
with that poem that is bigger on the inside
than on the outside?

Do you have the one
- you must have it -
with that poem that is a Library in itself,
each leaf a life we might one day live?

I don't know what it's called
but it calls, it calls.

Channelling Yourself

Cowgate

Andrew Blair

Into the valley we skid
Sober footed amid
Spillage idiom idiot spatter
Lads lads lads
Flowing is the order of day
Turns to night and says
Where do we go from here?
This:
Little island
(Distantly Hibernian)
Teeming and garish gauntlet
The thinking person's mood enhancer
Excuse me mate
Wrong
But still
All things must pass
We halt nostalgia pricks
Our conscience
We once swayed
On all sides of these detuned walls
That thrum delirious stars
Turn into the right of passage
Print explicit content in chips and cheese
Duck as stags' bawdy antlers thrust
Henward matched
By deely boppers
And abandon
This is freedom
Do you have ID?

Of course
These are our truest selves
Emerging from
Opium induced stupors
Imported percussion
And all around us
Human bridges
In various
States

A Pocketful of Posies

Greyfriars Kirkyard

Aileen Ballantyne

I will walk beside you,
insinuate, mutate:
Staphylococcus,
Simian, Bovine –
I can jump across –

SIV to HIV,
the lavender's blue
of Spanish flu –
Heliotrope Cyanosis –
I was here before you.

I watch you as you love,
copulate, beget,
insinuate, mutate.

I watch you as you're born,
watch you as they cleanse you,
a-tishoo, a-tishoo,
I watch as they bless you.

Scrape off a cell from your cheek,
write out a blueprint that's perfectly you,

magnify me, amplify me,
search my DNA,
sing a ring o' roses,
husha, husha:
hear the children play –

I was here before you.
You think that if you name me
I will go away?

Behind the scenes

Bedlam Theatre

Christine De Luca

The good doctor fretted over Fergusson, determined
none should suffer in a Poor House or a Mad House.
A good diet would build them up: porridge, broth
and mutton meals; and plenty exercise of course.
It took 40 years to assuage that poet's death, to found
the hospital for those whose mental health was fragile;
and 30 more before those Bedlam doors were closed.
Just as inmates left for Morningside, a striking kirk
ship-shaped that Bristo corner, too late to be of help.
No psalm will greet you now, no elder shake your hand
at the red door; a fellow student may welcome you, ask
your mission, whether acting, lighting, sound. Step inside!
Learn the ropes here, join the illustrious band of Bedlamites.
Lose and find yourself; work a different kind of healing.

Pre-Retirement Course

Riddle's Court

Anne Hay

This ceiling's spied birling ideas
beneath its chandeliers,
and carries codes: merchants,
murderers, leaves and rivers,
rosettes, caduceus, saltires,
skull and crossbones. Below,

space for fantasies to dance
till they settle on
This is how it's going to be.
For now, ciaroscuro: a too-white diary,
the last dark commute, an abrasive colleague
missed. A spooling back of lives lived
and unlived, hard-won lesson on
What gets you through. Vivendo Discimus:
By living we learn.

At close, no-one moves.
Someone shouts in the courtyard.
A drone of Old Town traffic.

Candlemaker Row

Greyfriars

Jane Alexander

The streets are just as they should be; which surprises me every time. I'm at the Haymarket junction, the train station in front of me, the Hearts memorial clock at my back, and to my right the main road running out of city. With a southwest wind, here's where you'd catch it: that sweet spot equidistant from the North British Distillery and the Caledonian Brewery. But we have no wind, of course, not yet – though the skin team are working on it, because how can we call it Edinburgh without a brisk southwesterly?

With no carrying breeze, I turn my head, tilt it; feeling for the right angle. I take a couple of cautious steps, trusting Marek to steer me away from obstacles. It ought to be easier than this. 'Still elusive,' I say. My voice sounds blunt and distant.

There. I catch it: hold the angle, inhaling carefully. 'Much better, now,' I say. 'But … still too thin. Too flat.' It has to be alive, this smell. Yeasty and bubbling. I wrinkle my nose. 'Top note of dust. Stale white bread.' I'm trying to taste what's missing. Something rich, and tangy. 'Marek … you know the frequency we're using for the Nor' Loch? Can you adjust the signals in that direction – just a tiny, tiny bit?'

The tweaks will take him a couple of minutes. I could do it quicker, but first I'd have to shed all the gear – the headset, the gloves, the mouthpiece – and that would take longer in the end. So I wait, instead, at the junction which is just as it should be – and yet, not quite. This was a transport interchange, constant with buses and trams, with trains and taxis and cars; above all, with people. And there will be people after we launch – all our users, interacting. Right now, though, the streets are static, silent. It could be crack of dawn on a Sunday morning, if the sun wasn't centred above me.

'Ah, Jesus!' A sudden nauseous stink overwhelms me. I cough and retch as I swipe for the touchpad, my gloved hands clumsy. The headset gets caught in my hair as Marek manoeuvres it off – and I'm blinking, back in the strip-lit lab. I use my tongue to pop the mouthpiece free, and spit it out onto my lap. 'Water!' I say, holding up my robot mitts. Marek eases the gloves off, lays them neatly on the trolley before handing me a bottle. I gulp, swooshing away the lingering, rancid smell.

'Too much?' says Marek.

'Just a bit.' I shake my head as he starts to apologise. 'Don't worry. Trial and error.'

'Do you want to tweak it? Try again?'

A flatness in his voice makes me glance up, check the time. It's late – after seven. I know Marek has a new baby daughter at home, a girlfriend counting the minutes. I also know he'll stay on, if I ask him to. I hesitate. Just one more try wouldn't take us long, and we're so nearly there. But then I think of Candlemaker Row. How close it is.

'Let's leave it,' I say, casually. 'Come fresh to it tomorrow.'

When Marek is gone, I rinse the mouthpiece, lay it aside for sterilisation. I should eat something, but that appalling smell has stolen my appetite. I'll never be hungry again. I glance at the frequencies he used, note down some adjustments to try later on. I could get away with what we've got, I'm sure – but it has to be right. Of all the olfactory details, this is the one we'll be judged on. This is the one that says Edinburgh. Remember, the first time we smelled it? Late September: the coach nosing its way towards the city centre, and the smell so warm, so thick I could practically chew it. Remember, I pulled a face, and buried my nose in your shoulder; it didn't yet mean home.

I run my gaze down the Gantt chart, admiring the ticks that show how many smells we've recreated. Roasting coffee from the police-box kiosks; fresh cut grass for the Meadows; the damp, closed smell of underground Edinburgh, its vaults and buried streets. My ghost smells are coming along, too: cocoa and rubber from the Fountainbridge factories; and for Princes Street Gardens, a faint reminder of the Nor' Loch, its previous life as the city's cesspit.

One day we'll have ghost people alongside my ghost smells. The technology isn't there yet – but when it is, we'll start with the old favourites: Mary Queen of Scots, Deacon Brodie, Robert Louis Stevenson. You'd roll your eyes at that: history for tourists. But how perfect to bring them back, the lives that were layered into this city. And we have to start somewhere.

Half past seven. If I time it right, I'll catch Rob on his own for a progress update. I loop my pass around my neck, and leave my basement lair.

The ground floor is deserted, silent but for the hum of the vending machine. Its lighted window draws me in; I decide I'm hungry after all. The machine offers me its last remaining sandwich, pushes it forward, lets it drop. Egg mayonnaise. I take it, and carry on upstairs.

In the first floor studio, glowing screens show where a handful of people are working late. There are more of us, usually. Those for whom it's a labour of love. Who lost the lot, when it happened; lost more than a home. More than a repository of memories. I wander from section to empty section – and then I realise. It's Friday night. Everyone else is tucked up with their families, or out on the town with friends.

Instead of turning back on myself, I press deeper into the studio. I didn't mean to grow attached to this workspace that's half science lab, half art school, but I find a sense of purpose here that's absent from anywhere else. A sense of necessary, urgent invention.

Perhaps some of the urgency comes from the pictures. In my

little lab, there's nothing to see. Grey benches, metal shelving, all my bits and bobs stored neatly in plastic tubs. What we're creating, Marek and I, it has no external reference, no source material. But here… Sometimes it feels like walking through a brighter version of my own head. Sometimes, it's like walking through wreckage.

In the aftermath, the internet buckled under the weight of memories. It was a tidal wave, millions of people all desperately remembering. Sharing whatever they had, in the hope that sharing would keep it alive. A lot of it was holiday snaps: the predictable route from castle to palace; the classic glimpse of New Town elegance through the dark of an Old Town close. Or cameraphone footage: from Calton Hill, the shaky 360 degrees of city… hills… sea… Visitors' Edinburgh, a tourist fantasy. That's what you used to say. You dismissed it, said it wasn't real. You were right, in a way: it was just too beautiful, too heart-stoppingly beautiful, to exist. Perhaps it never did: perhaps we dreamed it. A thousand-year consensual hallucination.

And now here we are – programmers and designers, scientists and sound artists, engineers and animators – all trying our hardest to dream it back.

There was other stuff too, in the tide of images. Architects' drawings. City masterplans. Slowly, people began to piece it all together: interactive maps, 3D simulations. Google Earth filled a lot of gaps. A call went out for the overlooked spaces. Thornybauk. Chuckie Pend. And when our project was set up – the Edinburgh Reboot – we gathered it all in.

Each team works on a different section, so as I wander the studio I'm walking through a mad jigsaw: the Canongate bumped up against the Meadows, the Cowgate leading to Moray Crescent. And in some of the photos are people. People like you, mostly. Dead people. I look back in time at a disaster that's yet to happen; the way the road speeds towards you and vanishes at the same time in the rearview mirror.

At first I think Rob's gone home for the weekend. His section is dark, lights and screens powered down. It's the smell that alerts me: malted barley, faint cousin of the aroma I've been struggling with. Then I see him, slumped at his desk, hand wrapped round an open beer.

'Alright?' he says, tipping the bottle towards me. 'Want one?'

'Yeah, sure.' I perch on the desk opposite his, click the Anglepoise on, and rip open my sandwich. 'D'you mind if I eat this? Can't downstairs; it's too eggy.' It's true: even a packet of crisps, an instant coffee, could taint the air for hours. When Marek first started working with me, I gave him a present of fragrance-free deodorant and unscented washing powder.

I lift my bottle: 'Cheers.' In the sharply-angled light, Rob looks knackered, his face criss-crossed with deep dark lines. 'What are we celebrating?' I say. 'Just, Friday night?'

He smiles. Shakes his head. 'It's finished,' he says.

I swallow. Put down my sandwich. 'Seriously?'

'I mean, there'll be snagging, obviously, but…' He raises his fist, like he'd be punching the air if only he had the energy.

'Wow. Well done, you must be… this should be champagne!'

'Yeah well, hopefully it'll get Kate off my back for a bit.'

I nod. His team have been running behind schedule, and everyone says it's not his fault. It's a difficult section of the city – small, but difficult. Different levels, sharp angles. The way it all fits together. 'She seen it yet?' I say, and he shakes his head.

'Monday.'

My mouth is dry; I take a swig of beer. Hear myself asking: 'Need a walk-through first?'

Rob straightens up in his chair, looks around at the empty office. 'Ah, no I couldn't ask you to. What time is it, past eight? You'll be wanting to get home.'

I set the bottle down. The glass clinking on the desk makes a definite sound. I know how much he needs this. A lot of the staff were never in Edinburgh; some visited once, for a week in August. So people like me, whose lives were there, we're in demand for walk-throughs. Team leaders tend to approach me cautiously – but I've always said yes, and I've always been professional. If I've ever needed to cry – if, for instance, they've asked me to test the Water of Leith from Stockbridge to Roseburn, and I've walked in the vanished footsteps of our Sunday strolls, walked all the way along with my hand closed round the absence of yours – then I've swallowed my loss; made my report on the authenticity of the terrain; locked myself in the disabled toilet before I fall apart.

'Honestly,' I say. 'I'm dying to see it.'

The testing room is blindingly bright after the dark of the studio. I've swapped my trainers for stability shoes, laced them up tight; on the platform, I slot my feet into place. I strap on the support belt and attach it to the safety ring, then Rob helps me on with the rest of the kit: the gloves, the headset. When he settles the headphones over my ears, I can hear my blood thumping.

'I'm actually kind of nervous,' he says.

'Me too.' But I say it softly, and I'm not sure whether he hears.

The first thing is, the light is wrong. Twilight setting: no good for a walk-through. I should swipe out, ask Rob to change it. But then my eyes adjust and I see that it's been raining; and I think how long it's been waiting for me, this place. Over my shoulder squats Castle Rock, built from code and light, pinning the Grassmarket by the tail under its great rugged weight.

I tilt my head back to see what they've done with the sky. Dull, pinkish clouds are tugging across the darkening blue, blown by a wind that doesn't touch me. As I watch, the clouds pull apart to reveal a two-thirds moon. How long would I have to crane upwards to notice the repeat – the exact same moment looped round again? But they've done a good job; I haven't seen a sky like this before. No wonder it's taken so long.

I start to walk. Streetlights spill across the wet stone flags, which change to setts under my feet, and back to roughened flagstones. The familiar pubs line the north side of the square, their faces just right – and I'm caught in a sudden wash of music, of voices and laughter, as though a door has opened briefly, as though there are lives inside. The Black Bull. The White Hart. The Last Drop. My chest feels tight. I walk on, past the gallows memorial. Here, by the chip shop, is where I'll place the stale fat and vinegar tang. Here, by the dark arched mouth of the Cowgate, is where I'll streak the air with a trace of urine, that faint Friday-night sweetness.

I'm climbing now, up Candlemaker Row. Past the high walls of the kirkyard, the odd assortment of shops, past Deadhead and Transreal and the tattoo parlour. My breath coming faster, legs working harder, as if I really am walking uphill. And when I reach the top of the street, I stop.

Four floors up: that's us. They've made the tenements too tall, the roofs blurring into the stone-coloured sky, so our flat's too distant from me. But it's the only one with a light on. A coincidence, a random choice by Rob or one of his team. I find myself thinking it's lucky we stayed central, weren't lured to suburbs that will never be rebooted, that we stayed tucked up in our crows-nest flat. Except of course if we had moved out, gone far enough from the centre, you and I would be there still. A twisted kind of luck, then. The same luck that meant I was away when it happened: travelling home on a train that shuddered to a halt somewhere outside Berwick, sat stranded while the news blazed through the carriages: impossible, incomprehensible.

Our window glows. Inside, in the kitchen, you'd be cooking, keeping an eye on the time: my train would be getting in soon, and it's a ten minute walk from Waverley, and you'd want to have dinner ready. You want to welcome me back.

I cross the road.

The familiar black of our front door. The cold stone lintel.

The handle, smooth against my palm. I grasp it. Turn it. Press my weight against the door, and push.

Nothing happens. Of course. Nothing can happen. There is no inside. If the door could move, it would only swing open to absence.

I hear my name – and just for a moment, I let myself believe. You're calling me. You have the sash drawn up, and you're leaning out, looking down at me. You think I must have forgotten my keys, and that's why I'm waiting. That's why I'm stuck outside.

Rob calls again. He wants to know, is something wrong? Has it frozen? Do I need a restart? Everything's fine, I tell him. Turn around, and cross the street once more.

I start to think of what's missing, what's not quite right; turning in a slow circle, trying to do my job. I let my gaze sweep loosely over spires and blocks and towers – and there's something wrong about the angles, or I think so at first – but then, how could I remember? How could I be expected to remember? Chances are he's got it right – Rob, who never lived here, who didn't know these walls, these stones, this sky. With all his source material, chances are his version is truer than mine. I can't keep it all inside. Not forever.

I carry on turning. The small silhouette of Greyfriars Bobby, endlessly waiting on his plinth, too daft to understand the finality of death. I walk around to the front of the statue to check his nose. I can't fault it: shiny, brassy as if from all the hands that have rubbed it for luck.

I rest the tips of my fingers against the worn bronze.

'Stupid animal,' I say.

I raise my hand towards the touch panel, ready to come out.

That's when I see it. A flicker, up at the kitchen window: like someone moving behind the glass, crossing the room.

'Rob—' I say, and my voice sounds panicked and then I press my lips shut. In the time it takes to refocus, the movement has gone. All that's shifted is the air. In the back of my throat I taste it, something hollow and deep. A gaping smell of damp and dust.

I can hear Rob in the other world asking what's the matter, but I tune him out. I call your name instead: in silence, inside me. I call you like a summons.

If I wait long enough, I'll see the repeat, the exact same glitch come round again. Or I'll see you cross the room, come to the glass and look in my direction.

You have to start somewhere; that's why we're rebuilding – but it's not the smell of the brewery that means home. It's not this dreamed, split-level city. It's not the glowing window in the gathering dark. All of this was only ever a frame.

I stare, trying not to blink. Breathe cold earth and stone. Wait, for the flicker against the light.

Greyfriars Bobby

Candlemaker Row

Jane Goldman

now
touched
for luck
like Montaigne's foot
    his bronze cast nose
      all rubbed
        down
      to its shiny
      still it pierces

      the dreich

        this dis-
      appearing
      slowly nose

        our very
      beacon of

      the virtual

      subjectivity

      of pethood

Tuning Up

Sandy Bell's

Richie McCaffery

Three fiddles are tuning up in Sandy Bell's
when one player cinches-in their chair
to be closer to the table and conversation.

The noise of this old wood rubbing against
the much-scuffed orange floor tiles makes
a note stronger than horse-mane and strings.

It is the sound of someone contented, taking
the place they choose, a clarion call against
the night that rubs its fur on the windows.

The Barrel Ride

The Scotch Whisky Experience

Tim Craven

The tours began early
so a decadent breakfast dram
could signal the intent
of a father's vacation as he absorbed
enough facts to amaze the regulars
back in the local: phenol content
and sherry influence,
the mouthfeel nuance imparted
by worm tub condensers
versus shell-and-tube,
importance of lyne arm angle,
honeyed sunrises and stewed fruits;
each region represented
like the top shelf of Heaven's
best stocked off-licence.
All without venturing beyond
the Central Belt. A plastic barrel ride
tracked back through a few hundred years
across a windswept strath sculpted
from reseda-green felt,
Blu Tack and pipe cleaners,
past animatronic Highlanders
stooped over a pot still, staring into it
as though it were a crystal ball,
illegally converting the harvest's
unconsumed excess into a spirit
that would thaw the winter
right out of their slow robotic bones.

Ghazal for the Camera Obscura

Camera Obscura

Rachel Plummer

All things bend towards it – even light.
The roads refract through urban space like light.

You can't help but approach it. City's eye
above the skyline, cloud eye, house of light.

The castle is a mirror. Its east side
reflecting Royal Mile is old-town-light.

Bask in it. Photons hail on brickwork, bright
with colour. See yourself distorted. Light

is loyal, it will follow you inside
where light blooming from bulbs is tulip light.

Remind yourself that some things are not quite
as they appear. This light is trickster light,

is hologram and hall of mirror, white
lie light. It might be infinite, this light.

It might be quicker than you know. So climb
above it, up to slate-tiled rooftop light

where nothing is obscured. The camera's eye
is witness to our city's many lights:

the photons that find stone from stone at night
when buslight lights North Bridge are citylight,

while shoppers on the new town pavements fight
a slow-flow tide of bloated bagpipe light

and particles of lightdust drift down side
streets northwards to the docks – this is Leithlight.

The wave of it that tumbles with the tide
into the Firth of Forth is waterlight;

the camera sees this far and further, out
to where the hills hoard old volcano light.

You hold it in your hand and in your eye,
this star-sent undulation we call light.

Rachel, you're the pinhole, picture, light
of Edinburgh's reflection – living light.

Exceptional Knowledge

Witches Memorial

Alice Tarbuck

Some Used Their Exceptional / Knowledge For Evil Purposes While Others Were /
Misunderstood And Wished Their Kind Nothing / But Good.

—Witches Well Memorial Text

Exceptional knowledge is the moment you
sit in the kitchen with your own two hands,
understand that nobody else is coming, understand
it's use them or get nothing.

Exceptional knowledge is the form
of your unwanted noticing:
which blood-backed coughs will stick,
which cows are falling ill,
and when they will get worse.
>   a curse is cast by speaking out, a curse
>   is cast by keeping your mouth still.

Do you know how grubby and small it is, this life?
Hygeia and Aesclepius can take a hike, wait it out
by Surgeon's Hall, let the rest get on with colds
and babies, ordinary mortal business
>   trying your best then going up in flames.

Have any of us ever wished our kind
nothing but good? Have any of us never thought
I'll put a limp in your gait, I'll bury your name deep,
I'll damp your woodpile, stamp your embers, steal
your sleep, your coin, I'll send you lice,
I'll drown your bloody ship, your bloody wife.

Burnt girls don't need live men's words
to speculate their good intentions:
they need witnesses against forgetting,
they need graves so we can bring
libations, so they never thirst again.

Love Poem to The Scottish Parliament
Scottish Parliament

Lady Red Ego

I've always liked Scottish girls.
And you know it, show it,
wear heritage beneath your clothes.
Your sprawling white body, your
reflective freckles. Sunless skin
that peels, highlight like the wings
of a beetle. In a country this grey,
you need a lot of windows.

We all grow into our bodies.
Mine is yellow, but I like your pale –
and aren't you also mixed? Traditional
and futuristic, you would not exist
if it weren't for forward flow.
You would like to have grown
from the land, but neither of us
own our homes.

Only love is organic. I like
your shapes, your swirls.
You have leaves like a tree,
branches like concrete, and could carry
a citizen across the sea. Immigrate
into the future. Tell me you
won't leave.

How I Met your Grandad

Assembly Rooms Dance Hall, Constitution Street

Stephanie Green

'Are ye dancin'?' You bet. I lived
for the Rooms: the smell of Brylcreem,
after-shave, hairspray and floor polish; spangles
of light from the glitter-ball trawling the crowds.

Girls in beehives, teetering high heels,
stick-out petticoats stiffened in sugar water;
 D.A.s and quiffs were O.K. but Teddy Boys
were banned, jackets measured at the door.

It took courage for boys to cross the wastes
of sprung floor. Would they be snubbed?
Being a wallflower was no fun either
and a girl who said No had to sit the dance out.

We quick-stepped, jitterbugged, cha-cha'd and tangoed
the night away. Some of us could even foxtrot.
Boys had to learn or be stranded halfway through.
The jive would get you barred for three months.

 Alexander's band could play anything,
ragtime to Bill Haley. You could smooch
to Glenn Miller's: 'In the Mood' or go wild
to 'Chattanooga- choo-choo'.

At the break, it was soft fizzy drinks
or tea, the spoons chained to the counter.
A kiss on the cheek. None of that.
Kiss Killers roamed to make sure.

The waltz for slow numbers, more
of a shuffle, was always the Last Dance.
He had to be tall. No shorties.
You didn't want his nose in your bra.

And it meant he got to walk me home.
Trusting a stranger, a bit shocking maybe
But I had to be back by midnight
or else. Mam was waiting up.

A Brief History of Earth

Our Dynamic Earth

Alycia Pirmohamed

If I look back far enough, the earth
blossoms from the sun's mouth—

        half language, half light—

4400 million years ago, the first skirt of ocean
pleated with rain and rain and rain and

I read scrolls of mist slung over mountains,
the script of volcanos, the *drop drop*

drop over bodies woven like rivers.

If I look back far enough, there is the shape
of our first breath—

        rod and ellipsoidal—

pools of algae that become
the soft belly of words like heart and meadow,

and forests tracing back their faces
to the origin of bloom.

I follow this timeline from slenderdark fish
to the moment of speckle and dust,

the ancestor of my ancestors, the ancient
story of rock and water.

South

Enunciation

Roseneath Terrace

Peter Mackay

I never dreamt of living here
in 19th century Roseneath stone.
The tenement steps are worn
through the grain, and strain

into the wall, the whole building
cantilevered. As it were.
Invisible to the eye, the weight-
bearing loads are a partial proof

of the existence of God. The steps
seem to tremble in the air,
as we watch feet pass above us,
in and out of time, against the unseemly

persistence of stone. These feet now,
leather-bound, belong to a toga party:
tanned shoulders and bare backs,
heady, giggly, white sheets held up

by Sellotape, hidden pins
and bravado. Some other time
these will be sheets for ghosts,
holes cut for their eyes,

but today they are Romans,
confident in their enunciation.
White flocked cotton brushes rose sandstone.
They might live forever.

a crossroads

Holy Corner

Aonghas MacNeacail

there is a grandeur, though not
obtrusive, in those old stone silences
that stand as sentry towers

each, should you wish to enter,
would benignly offer you
its own distinctive password –

that there are four, all bearing
the insignia of their particular
refinements of the creed they share

does not impose a diktat on those
citizens who pass, *en route* to what
must be attended to – they do not

even ask for prayers to be spoken
in their name, they have the solid
certainty of being, and doors to open –

they can offer shade and shelter,
being there to pass or enter – take
or leave, each offers welcome

You Can't Cut Fat From A Hand

Wester Hailes

Sophie Cooke

Here's where they took the stone
Edinburgh's New Town was built from –
all those grand Crescents, and Places,
the cosy cafes, the delis – their foundations
cut from Hailes Quarry.

Here's where the Council put the people
who'd been living in leaking slums,
to save them, in 1971. A new town
made in concrete, built on farmland.

Car parks, for folk without cars –
though nowhere to shop.
No insulation: cheap, prefabricated walls.
Water ran down the insides of the rooms,
dripped down behind the beds.

When you build a grand idea
for other folk to live with,
remember –
what's not good enough for you
isn't good enough for them.
What isn't good enough will be destroyed,
or altered, by dynamite and dust clouds,
or women with trowels, stamps and pens.

Now there are shops. A canal, swans,
trees and footpaths. But it's hard to walk
with your face always into the wind.

Life is different
if your stone's been quarried out
so you've nothing to fall back on –
if a setback can be a real disaster.
Sometimes, the wind can make your eyes water.
Imagine
a life with insulation.

Western Town
Springvalley Gardens

Ryan Van Winkle

To be lonely – set yourself west, build a town
where the sun's not yellow, it's chicken.

Keep a shirt there, pockmarked,
long sleeved. Knock

at doors – wait and then wait –
or maybe just shoulder in, swing them

out of tune, a creaking saloon piano.
Put a horse in it – and Old Susanna

coming round the mountain. Wait
for her to arrive – wear your wet pistol,

your foggy coat, your boots with a whiff
of hay – tumbleweeds swaggering down,

taking it easy, on the ghost dust road.
Indivisible, rugged – can't buy a thrill – souls.

Asylum

Morningside

Helen Boden

The Number 5,
The Morningside Maisie,
off towards RLS's hills of home,
slips past bad parking
charity and artisan shops
on the resurfaced 702. Between
Waitrose and the Pizza Express
with Jean Brodie quotes
on its walls: Morningside Road,
route and destination.

> In hinterlands that tessellate
> with Comiston, Craighouse, Merchiston,
> Churchhill, Blackford, Grange:
> stone villas; the salubrious
> hospital parks. Ashley Ainslie,
> Royal Ed. We all know someone
> who's been inside.

between

> its northern boundary ruled
> by the elongated back facade of Watson's
> and where the suburban railway
> underscores the southern end

know

how the psychiatric-hospital mythology
resonates through neighbourhoods
well beyond these grounds.

The site map lacks a You Are Here.
Its Red, Green, Blue walking routes
confuse. So many dead ends
you can't get round the periphery,
have to walk on the grass,
find passages through gaps

                    between clinics, wards and units
                    – Cullen – Rivers – Fergusson –
                    on the outskirts of a city
                    that knows how to commemorate.

Three centuries' mixed media:
clapboard, sandstone
balustrades and redbrick.
Repurposed and purpose-built.
High rise. Low rise. Ill-advised additions.

                    On hedge-partitioned lawns
                    of the original mansions in-
                    patients make gardens
                    and grow their own,
                    paint welcome signs promoting
                    dignity – contribution – skills
                    in free-form defiance
                    of the NHS house style
                    for Laundry, Catering, Estates.

The pathway to the orchard
has a padlocked barrier
while the site is extended with the latest newbuild.

Thaw drips from trees. It sounds like rain.
Two magpies squabble at the end of the carpark
competing with rugger calls from the playground at
Watson's.
Beyond the asphalt a rabbit jumps
from a camouflage of dead leaves and chippings.

                    Back on the main drag, the homeless woman
                    who sits outside Oxfam and always says hello,
                    whose name I never got round to asking, isn't
                                    there.

What Ruby Learned at University

Napier University

Patricia Ace

(for Ruby, after Kate Bingham)

How to compose a song in strophic form.
How to live with other people; how to be alone.
The difference between a melodic and harmonic scale.
How to thrive on value coffee, rum and cereal.
How to make a morning lecture after dancing until five.
How to shoot Sambuca. How to get high.

How to find her way around the fretboard of a bass.
When to keep her counsel, when to seek advice.
That the No. 16 takes the most scenic route.
How to give blood. How to play a duet.
How to talk to God on the big white telephone.
How to keep a secret. When to keep on keeping on.

How to write a lyric. How to file her tax.
What other people sound like when they're having sex.
How to down a pint in one in Henry's Cellar Bar.
How to throw a party. How to volunteer.
When to call a doctor. How to beat the cliques.
How to procrastinate and prioritise. How to find a niche.

Nowhere special

The Royal Observatory

Pippa Goldschmidt

*The guiding principle of astronomy is the Copernican Principle – what we
see from Earth could (over large distances) be seen from anywhere else.*

My first lesson was to learn the unreliability of stars
each night I calculated the odds against seeing them
in a sky loaded with possible rain.

Dusk brought with it illuminations
unwavering and yellow
sodium was
the most dependable light.

My second lesson was the Copernican principle
"I am not special"
a verb to be learnt
and conjugated for my supervisors.

No matter, they said,
don't mind the streetlights
you can study the invisible
the dark road between them
better study that, girl
better study the way out
the road that leads away from here because
"You are not special"
but I came here to map the sky
to search for the absolute truth.

The third lesson
"he is not special"
well, he was special
but only because I made him that way
he knew how to solve the great equations
he measured space so accurately
a pin's width between his number and the truth
so I thought he wanted to answer
the silent questions I could not stop asking
Am I not at the centre of my own life?
If not, then where am I?

I was wrong
this was my next lesson
(I stopped counting now)

I was young enough to be awkward
and to think of it as a youthful thing
I was young enough to flick the switch
electrify the sleeping body
shine the interrogator's light on the dreaming sky.

Repeat after me
"We are not special"

After he receded
the blue aftershock observed
when the sirens flashed past
the body inside the ambulance
conveyed to another place
beyond my reach
off the edge of my map
I made a dodge away from the Universe.

It wasn't precisely a retreat from the territory
I don't know why I did it – exactly
maybe it was a retrograde motion
they didn't teach me insight at the Observatory.

The therapist said *Be here now, be mindful*
and I said *The Universe is matter, not mind*
I had learnt all my lessons, you see.

Some people just can't help taking
the Copernican principle too much to heart
we are the natural observers
on the edge of the city
but still we can learn to move
and to be moved.

Getting to Heriot-Watt

Heriot-Watt University

Jonathan Bay

We didn't look up the Google images
We didn't anticipate the hill-shaped sky, always falling
We didn't understand the lay of Scottish land
We didn't trust the end of the bus line, so we practised
We didn't expect the glass and brick
We didn't want our feet to walk until these paths were familiar
We didn't know the sandstone statue would be so downcast
We didn't expect to fin d comfort in rhododendrons
We didn't trust a year to make a difference

Getting lost in the physics department

King's Buildings

Pippa Goldschmidt

The password for this building is
unify
to get inside, you must want to hook together
those subjects which (on the surface) appear separate:
apple to moon
light to radio
electron to 'electron'.

But after I'm allowed to enter
these are the only truths I can discover:
the corridors feel endless
the room numbers are random
and I am lost –
picture me as a scribble of lines on a graph.

The transformations we're searching for
aren't carbon-13 to carbon-14
or base metal to gold
but these –
the pencil marks
that write the world in symbols
and a short poem about a long building.

Winter Solstice at the Secret Herb Garden

The Secret Herb Garden

Patricia Ace

(for Muriel Nairn)

There's many a herb to cure,
Not one, however, for death, to be sure.

Here, in the glasshouse,
the plants overwinter:
camomile and mint drowse;
rough clumps of lavender

sprawl in unkempt beds.
Rosemary leaves, star-like,
smell of balm a mother spreads
on an ill child's chest at night.

Here's lemon verbena,
its citrussy leaves aromatic;
sage, the sick-room cleanser;
milk thistle, a liver tonic.

Winter jasmine twines
through willow pea cones;
grapes flinch on vines
against the stinging cold.

All is in abeyance.
Yet here are cures
for all our ailments –
for loneliness, for terror;
for those who suffer dread

of illness, the dark, of poverty
with gentle forbearance instead,
when there is no remedy.

All these leaves weary, yellowing.
Yet rubbed between fingers
their scent clings to the skin,
still potent, tenacious.

Edge of Edinburgh

Redford and Dreghorn Barracks

Helen Boden

Redford and Dreghorn: the capital's
allium capitals – it hardly counts as
foraging, when ingredients for pesto
are prolific as strimmers in the gardens
of the four-in-a-blocks across the burn.
She's taught herself to hear
traffic on the bypass as a river in spate,
convinced herself the noise of firearm practice
from the barracks beside the woods
comes from something more benign,
more colourful than artillery.
After all, this city needs little excuse
to stage another firework display.
And here on its periphery,
the army have their own parties,
for summer fairs and Hogmanays
and ends of tours of duty – though since
the Stade de France and Bataclan
she's thought more of reaction times:
how you tell when something isn't
entertainment, isn't background noise.

She thinks of Owen writing home
on admission to Craiglockhart: 'I am
just going out to get the lie of the land' –
its end-of-season ramsons Dell
its own version of the Sambre-Oise canal,

its training trenches above the cavalry stables.
He'd be discharged before spring came again
in the Dreghorn woodlands; he wouldn't snap
the stems of invasive, grassier, more pungent
allium paradoxum, few-flowered leek.

Crossing the Meadows

The Meadows

Marjorie Lotfi Gill

This clearing of sky takes
a knife to the edge of town,
lops off its scraggled end:
that old record store with bins
and a plastic man chained
to the front door grinning
at the red hot and blue
tattooed girl, the queue
of second hand bicycles
wet in wind for want
of a rider. If you like, use
twilight to blunt
the city's tail, the bit
as a kid you never wanted
to see from the car window;
you'll miss the breaking open
of empty space, its belly
zigzagged with concrete
and the arms of trees grazing
people rushing past, focused
only on getting from here
to there, failing to notice
the change in light.
I, for one, do not want
to cross this threshold,
and cannot tell you why.

Grassroots on the Meadows

The Meadows

Elizabeth Rimmer

(for Katherine Cameron)

There's so much surprising green in this city's grey
stone heart, so douce, so mercantile.
I miss that four pointed arch at Jawbone Walk
beyond the cherry trees, all pink and lyrical
under a wide spring sky, although the waste
of whaling still appals. There's grass here
for cyclists and joggers and barbeques,
teens making out, students with their books,
and no one sells you anything but thought.
Radical starts here, with all the marches –
stop climate change, ban trident, the white
ribbon we wrapped round Edinburgh
to make poverty history. I saw my first
feminist badge here – *the future is female* –
pink on the coat of a mother at the swings.
But most radical of all, on that March day
before Thatcher, in the winter of discontent,
when snow fell, and lay, and froze, and people
skied down Princes Street, we put on hiking boots
and crossed The Meadows to the Simpson,
last day of two, the day when you were born.

People's People

Grange Cemetery

Viccy Adams

The low wall in the back section of the Grange Cemetery was where she and James used to sit and wait for their parents to catch them up. Janet holds her gloves palm-down over the scabs where the council has picked the stone clean of moss, then smells them. Standing straight, she can see the spire of the church across the road from what used to be her grandparents' flat.

Ham on white, no tomato. Bums protected from the wet by plastic bags, slipping and rustling. Complaining that there were no crisps. Laughing at James as he tried to sound out the names on the Egyptian-style gravestones. Running so fast they never fell but they flew round fallen granite and over patchy mud. Unexpected bruises surfacing in the bath days later from the half-games of pushing and balancing along tomb boundaries.

One time, the time she remembers most, the bent-over man with a stick and tears in his eyes shaking and trembling as he hissed at them, 'There are people's people buried here, you know.'

Running away and neither of them mentioning it to Mam and Dad. Still, the rest of the summer holidays Janet had heard it in the wind through the pine trees and the repetition of the car tyres on the tarmac as they toured. *There are people's people buried here, you know.*

She turns her back and closes her eyes to let the birdsong and muted traffic seep in. The morning-cereal crunch of slow footsteps on gravel is followed by the fumble of a large gloved hand gripping hers. Janet knows that if she opens her eyes then she will see it again, that slick and clean headstone so shockingly pink. Far pinker than the granite had looked in the catalogue.

They both would have hated it. We made the wrong decision. How much would it cost to replace it?

*

Adam

Adam's hands are pushing deep into his pockets and he's turning his face out of the wind, away from her. He's telling her he doesn't see the point in them staying a second night at her parents' house; he has an essay to write he'd forgotten about, his books are back in Leeds.

Janet takes him off the path and onto the wet grass, slipping round the solid gold of crocuses and into one of the wide divots of the Bruntsfield Links.

She turns him sideways in the wind until there are tears in his eyes and he is facing the backside of the city.

He cannot see the old walls from here, but he can take in the wideness of the Meadows and agree to the existence of ancient boundaries.

She tells him they are off-limits, beyond the outskirts. The green heaves under their feet were formed by the decaying bodies of the dead in the limed mass graves hastily excavated and then rammed with cart-driven corpses from the plague-decimated closes off the Mile. 'And now it's a public golf course,' she fin ishes.

He blinks through the eye-filling wind, says he doesn't see anyone playing golf. Janet looks down to hide her face and she sees the stains tidal on his suede shoes from the wet grass she has brought him onto.

*

Michael

He really, really wants her to tell him what she thinks it must be like to *be* an extinct volcano. Janet's running out of ways

197

of saying that she doesn't know without him noticing that she doesn't care. A mid-afternoon stag party passes the plate glass window on their way to the next-door strip bar and one of them sticks his head in the half-open door and winks at her.

She's toying with the gold-rimmed vintage saucer of beetroot and chipotle cake that she wishes she hadn't ordered. Half an eye is on that group in the corner crowded round the closed lid of a piano, because if they do leave – which they might have done ages ago, had they any consideration for customers with full cups and plates – then she wouldn't have to balance like this by the till. In the meantime she pretends she is enjoying drinking the artisanal fla t white while standing up and being jostled by the queue.

He offers again to hold her coat – which is quite sweet really, when she thinks about it – and asks what time dinner is booked for.

'Seven. We're meeting at half six though. Dad has – well, you'll see. He has this thing about punctuality.'

'I'm really, really looking forward to meeting them,' Michael says. Janet sees the honesty shining out of his face and feels nothing but exhaustion.

*

April

'You could come on your own, sweetheart.' Her mother pauses opposite the city library to look over and down. Up ahead April is surrounded by a passing language school group admiring the full Escher's steps experience. 'James drops by all the time.'

Janet asks her mother to keep her voice down and links arms, pulls her closer, as if her body could block the words better than the blaring piper on the corner. 'He lives in Glasgow. It's hardly the same.'

'The spare room fits one just as well as two.'

They have already paced the tartan gauntlet of shops on the

Royal Mile and now they are to be paraded round Greyfriars
Bobby.

Over breakfast that morning, April trying to be polite.
There's no need to treat me like a tourist. Her father, unsmiling,
scraping marmalade on his toast. *You never know when you'll be
back in Auld Reekie.* So here they are, being passive-aggressively
chaperoned.

An earshot in front, her father is walking stiff-legged next
to April and lecturing her about how the statue of the wee dug
should be facing the other way, towards the graveyard and
his master's final resting place. His conspiracy theory about
brown-envelope payments from the pub to have it turned
around so the pub sign headlines tourist snaps.

April is promising not to take a photo, in mute protest.
Then the world is drowned by the horn of a taxi as Janet
steps out in front of of a loading bus. Her eyes lock into the
sudden stop of the taxi's windshield and the angry white of the
driver's knuckles on the steering wheel, peeking over his high
dashboard.

Then she is on the other side, stomach growling at the
smell of Italian cuisine from the vents in the sandstone wall
that April is pushing her into. All three of their voices – April,
her mother, her father – unified in scolding: *are you trying to
give me a heart-attack? Why do you never look where you're going?
What were you thinking?* And the odd, warm pleasure of being
their common concern, their common complaint.

*

Now her other hand is being gripped too, gloves twined by
those long, slender fingers. Red with the cold, she knows from
experience. She pulls their combined fist into her coat pocket,
awkwardly, while her brother coughs and hems and eventually
lets go of her other hand to blow his nose.

April is the first one to speak. 'Do you remember them

bringing me here, for the Sunday walk, that first time I was invited to join in?'

But the thing is, Janet doesn't. All those layers of memories, of people. Even as April goes on to talk about the sunshine and the warmth and the jokes, Janet is sifting her brain without success.

'We had a flask of tea, still too hot to drink when we stopped for lunch.' James is joining in and still nothing surfaces.

She opens her eyes and the two of them are looking at each other, smiling. Then she realises – she hadn't been there. The first time April was alone with her family, without her padding out the conversation and protecting them both from embarrassment. Janet stuck in the spare room with a bucket by the bed and a plate of water biscuits.

But April had gone out. The memory is thickening now, wiping over the cemetery like butter. Had come back rosy cheeked. *I think they like me. It was okay, really it was.* And it had been.

The sun goes behind the weather and the colour of the stone darkens, becomes less lurid. James and April start to walk round to the entrance, muttering about rain. Janet tells them she'll catch them up. Reaches out to wipe the top of the granite with her glove, brushing her parents' deep-cut names with her thumb. *There are people's people buried here, you know.*

Kelpie

Oxgangs

Rachel Plummer

Beside the pond, with honesty in her hair, a kelpie
scraped a hard hoof on the tarmac, and you followed her

past the plum trees, where slick orange
mushrooms bubbled from the path behind her;

through squat blocks of flats, where the ghosts
of the tower blocks hung like crows above you;

by the playpark, where at her breath the burnt swing suddenly
cooled, paled, and righted itself to swing healthily again;

across the football pitches, where the scars of fireworks
burst into clover and bees swarmed like blood cells;

past the white church, where the barred windows broke
from their metal cages and opened wide at her whinny;

through the chippy, where the smell of food was greater
than the smell of hunger, and out the other side;

to the big road, where the kelpie walked
through traffic as if nothing could touch her

and nothing touched her.

At a Reading, Summerhall

Snigdha Koirala

you burst yellow against days drawn-out
drenching craters the minute hand

and my left thumb   (bruised-crooked thumb)
(doing-time-with-the-bitter-cold thumb)

in the dimmed heat of this room
I forget   what I am / am I

meant to say   we laugh at the queue
of sheep   awake and hungry at the bar

words hemming their puffed silhouettes
they talk   we listen   years from now

they will write about my perpetual
fear of being consumed   how as

a girl   I'd spend hours unbriefing
my body   limb after limb

I wanted to last   like the air's breath
its exhale tonight   a pour over

your cheeks   a thought along your collar
ambrosial blue   like a berry

in the face of this predicament
I stumble upon

how to fold myself into
the night   violet-petaled   and coming

to an end   as the lines
on my page   begin to grow teeth

In Rosslyn Chapel

Rosslyn Chapel

Stella Birrell

Odin's jarlsmen
glum with foliage,
leaves caught like bridled bit
in stretched jaw, saddled
with the memory of
Cromwell's horses
stabled here, stamping
on the graves of Templar knights.

Pillars scarred by flaying chains,
then filled, sealed, cemented grey.
Where radiant cauliflower
fades to a suggestion of bronchioles.
A double-helix made murder ballad by keyholder
with an eye for a poet, an ear for a tale.

Angels play the bagpipes,
the lute, the fyfe and drum:
fairy doors, and keeps, and castles stand
open, are emptied out – the Pagan,
the Catholic and the Episcopalian
waiting for twelve o'clock prayers
all meet here.
Lucifer dangles silent, upside down,
snaked with rope.
The cat is real.

One wise monkey
(friends with camel, elephant, fox, lamb)
sits atop chamber pot
ready to piss down on England
in defiance, the auld alliance.
Death dances away from Bethlehem.
Two-hundred-year-old stained glass
and organ loft awkward –
hadn't realised the dress code was sandstone.

I lie on cushioned pew:
roof's garden of
wildflower meadow,
vegetable patch,
rose,
pentagon-hexagon-petalled forget-me-nots,
all ends
and all begins
with stars.

East

Deceit

Sherlock Holmes statue

Finola Scott

The giraffes are looking
worried, shifty even.
That guy's back, planted himself
above shoppers and frenzied traffic.

> Crossing from the Omni, you brush my hand
> *I can't go on like this.*

Sherlock tucks away his moleskin notebook,
footers with his pipe, wonders
if he left his cigars in the coal scuttle,
tobacco in the toe of a Persian slipper?

In deer-stalker and bronze cape
he's impervious to rumour or lies.
Today it's not cocaine or morphine.
But don't be fooled by hooded eyes.

You're a specimen. He observes
your coat for hairs – blonde or brunette?
Shoes for mud, or is it clay?
Face for telling marks – scars, tattoos, smudged lipstick.

> I stuff hands into pockets and feel
> tell-tale cinema stubs and bus tickets.

Enemies and agents are everywhere
but facts wait coiled at this tangled junction.

Ishtar on the Number 35

Easter Road

Kevin Cadwallender

From the window high above Easter Road
Christ knows who is playing the bagpipes
It drifts down to us like stereotypical haar

From the upstairs fla t two people are yelling
As children wail in a pitch that out-skirls the pipes
It washes over me, drowns the day.
The traffic whooshes and growls
Intent on destination and delivery.

They are digging up Easter Road
cutting into its elephant hide,
Vibrations carry through the walls,
Men in yellow jackets and white hats
are singing above ear defenders,
but you can't make out the words.
Easter Road will never forget.

The moon picks up the thread of daylight
Runs it through the needle of night,
Darns the holes left for closure
By starlight in the blanket height.

But these are not the days for lovers
Ô mes petites amoureuses,
    Que je vous hais!

Romeo and Juliet outplayed
By Leyla and Mejnun,

Who hold the tragic hand
In living's universal tragedy.

They walk through us all
Possess us, though we have no souls
To sing about, learning the words by rote
To redundant, moribund tunes.

They argue under the streetlight
She is soap opera drunk and he
Is Noah with his only sin intact.

Fade amas d'étoiles ratées
Sous les lunes particulières

   Mes laiderons!

The daybreak an arrest away,
They compromise as the police arrive.
And spend the night committed to
What passes for love in loveless climates.

Gaius Valerius Catullus
On his favourite hobby horse
Arm in arm with Helvius and Licinius
Stagger between the graves on Easter Road

Ah love her man, Ah really love her
But she's a feckin' cow…
We are all Cinnas
Torn apart by love
By poetry, our hearts' lyres
Plucked by harpies.
We are all sinners one shot short
Of glory, one goal behind victory.

The police horses coconut the tarmac Drop
fertiliser for the shared roses
Of back greens, Flack jackets
Ushering the away scarves
down Bothwell Street
(I had not known life had undone so many)
Towards the skinny metal bridge.
Graffiti on their tongues
Buckfast bards and too many
Eighty Shillings,
Pieces of malt and silver,
golden showers against the abandoned
B&Q waiting for resurrection as a Lidl.

… effin poufy words. Ah write mi ain,
Ah've got mi work on show all oor Leith.

The road sweeper wheels his cart
Into the sun that breaches the street
From Arthur's seat,
Picks up the debris of sport
Fulfils the hours of his debt,
A Hibernian shirt under his
Visibility vest, although he
Would wish to be invisible
And do his hours in peace.

It is necessary to see how the end of every affair turns out, for
the god promises fortune to many people and then utterly ruins
them.

In sudden contemptuous rain
She knocks at my door,
Says she cannot forget

Whilst choosing to ignore.

I thought that I would be immune
To this push and punishment of longing
While she takes too long to care
The turnstile of respect is closing.

I imagine this narrow road worn away
A slow erosion from the passing of feet,
cars, pedestrian ideals, other 'stuff'.
Repaired, patched up
every once in a while,
But still a residue of bird
and dog guano, vomit,
Languages, violent acts,
death and other exits.

People move in and out,
moving up to Morningside,
Climbing the pathetic ladder
of social class to Stockbridge
Slipping on supposed snakes
to Granton or Craigmillar
Slipping under the great
unjust system of privilege.
The day demands more
than polemic.

The sun flushes up the street
Followed by the rain,
Followed by the darkness
And the wait for sun again.

From a window high above Easter Road
she gazes with a child slung on one arm

looks for her lover who is in a doorway
with a cigarette, a lighter and another woman.

Her child is sleeping, taking the night
to its dreams and hiding even there.

He washes her perfume off his skin
in a pool of water in an empty park.

The dark is deciding
how to wear its shades.
Easter Road rises and shakes
dust from its tusks.

North Down Easter Road

Easter Road

Colin McGuire

A shoe halted over a twirl of shit,
narrowly missing detonation;
a gift left by an arthritic rottweiler.

A spaniel nosing for scent at a lamppost,
scanning for treasure, for a trace of urine,
some last territorial ember.

A toothless wonder; breath that could cut you in
half, poor story eyes, pressing for a pound to pocket:
'best bet's Princes Street, year round, brother.'

Blunt hardware traders, broke lads in Ladbrokes,
hirsute hairdressers, drug rehabilitators,
cancer survivors; unwitting troopers.

There's a graveyard half-hidden, half-unknown,
constantly flowering in colour, someone is tending
to the dead, even in winter the garden has its summer.

Easter Road stadium, new cup, ripe for the loyal,
who swear to God, and stamp his ground;
leave at the whistle, soldiers for a revolt that never starts.

The number 35 can break you out of here,
to Paris, Rio, Nova Scotia; anywhere,
so long as it's drenched in vitamin D weather.

In the end there is only the Persevere,
the last bar on the lip of the street;
a quick jar against sealed odds, for all you live.

Dreaming Spires

Leith Walk

Jane Yolen

'The graceful and powerful giraffes symbolise the
aspirations of a country which has often felt the
constraints of history and traditions, and now embraces
the opportunity to look beyond them.'– Helen Denerley

Helen's house in Strathdon
is lower than this lofty pair.
It spreads out beside a meadow
sweeping down to a burn,
where in the workshop, new, sunny,
drawings of deer, ready to flee the wall,
gaze past my shoulder.

Here the two giraffes began,
her own dreams thrusting her
suddenly into the future. She picked
leg bones, back bones, long necks
from the piles of old cars,
trucks, tractors, bikes
that burden the lawn.

And now they stand twenty-two feet
high over Leith Walk, a pair
aspiring into the shifting
Edinburgh air, into a future

overseen by tourists whose only dreams
were tartan, travel and a dram,
now dreaming a Scottish savanna,
where the heat rarely rises.

Benediction

Manuscript of Monte Cassino

Anne Connolly

Did the train at Leith Central Station
choo-choo harder on the day you were born,
its belly fired like the furnaces you'd use
to quicken your molten dreams mercurial
and mighty? Big Man at the Dean
with the stride of a Goliath. And Big Foot.
Now there's a wonder. Shoppers on their way
to Princes Street speculate at this conundrum.

On the one hand, and there is only one,
a pair of locusts propagate their greed.
The ravaging of Pharaoh's golden harvest. It
could be Zika, Dengue if the ancient script
were written for today. But then you grip the
orb with new genetic possibilities
forged deep and secretive. A way to beat
the beasties at their game or tweak
the double helix into some bizarre chimera?

So far from Benedict's simplicity
on the rocky rise beyond Cassino.
For guests there is abundance of garden herbs,
fish and bread. A welcome for the pilgrims
foot-weary, headed for Rome. Paolozzi's
roots transplanted to the plaza by St. Mary's
where steps rise in a broad sweep

their gradient worn by countless feet
still hoping for *a consecrated peace,*
lowliness of heart and uplifting harmony.

Some manuscript Mr Paolozzi!

Gallow lee

Leith Walk

Colin McGuire

Gallow Lee, literally the 'field with the gallows', where several infamous executions took place, near Leith Walk.

1697. Heads spiked above the city gates,
six witches' necks cracked like kernels in a kiln;
thieves roasted before an open crowd,
strangled first to spare the screams.

Bodies burned above the fagots, then buried
beneath the gibbet, holding out its proud arm
in salute: Leith Walk is breathtaking
in the afternoon. Imagine, true stories:

A young buck of twenty, hung for blasphemy.
Matriculated, fresh-arsed out of Uni; doubted God,
why not? doubted fie rcely and learnt it, dead.
Thomas Aikenhead, hung in silence – claimed his end.

Hereafter, it's the longest stretch down to the port,
out of this world. Streets lined with many a staggerer,
slugged by some cursed sniper. Mumbling through
the last of their blood as they totter, hugging grim walls.

Helen's Hair is closing up. Speyside lounge
has disco-balls glinting out of place
where there's barely room to really care.
Karaoke's booming proud. It floods the street

in all its noise; the sore sight glaring,
down at the miserable-end-of-drab
not some glam sing-song for laughs,
a last-chance bar, pavement stained with
puke.
Thin and cold, a diabolical night continuing
with sorcery and witchcraft, we palm our phones
speak drunk in tongues, take turns of personality,
paranoid lurches back towards where we came from.

Hauf-hingit Maggie

Sheep's Heid Inn, Duddingston

Gerda Stevenson

*(Margaret 'Maggie' Dickson, 1702 – 1765,
a salt-seller, from Musselburgh.)*

Daith is wappin whan it comes – like birth;
I ken – I hae warstled throu, an focht wi baith.
She wis blue, ma bairn, blue as the breist o a bird
I seen oan the banks o the Tweed thon day; then grey,
aa wrang, the naelstring windit ticht aroon her neck; I
ettled tae lowse it, aince, twice, but it aye slippit – ma
hauns couldnae grup, ma mind skailt
frae the jizzen fecht, ma mooth steekit:
no tae scraich, no tae scraich, lat nane hear…

I stottert oot, doon tae the watter, thocht tae douk her
in its cauld jaups, but ower late. I laid her quate
in lang reeds, achin tae hae a bit basket tae float her oot
like Moses, aa the wey tae England an the sea,
gie her a deep grave, ayont kennin; but they fund her,
still as a stane whaur she lay; an syne me,
wannert gyte agate Kelso toon. "Murther!"
they yaldered, "Murther!" like dugs.

Embro Tolbooth's a dowie jyle. An mercy? Nane they gied me
at ma trial – the verdict: hingin. The duimster slippit the towe
ower ma heid, drapt the flair – but I'd lowsed ma hauns,
I grupped thon raip, aince, twice, thrice at ma thrapple –
I'd dae it this time! The duimster duntit me wi his stick,
dunt, dunt, an the dirdum dinged in ma lugs,
"Clure the hure! Clure the hure!" Syne aa gaed daurk.

A chink o licht. The smell o wid, warm – a cuddie's pech;
ma een appen. I lift ma nieve, chap, chap oan ma mort-kist lid,
chap, chap! A scraich ootby, a craik o hinges. I heeze masel, slaw,
intil ma ain wake, at the Sheep Heid Inn. Fowk heuch an flee:
"A ghaist, a bogle, risin fae the deid!" I sclim oot, caum.
The braw brewster gies me a wink, hauns me a dram.
I sup lang the gowd maut, syne dauner back tae life, an hame.

Soul Mate

Arthur's Seat

Iyad Hayatleh

(For Tessa Ransford)

In her flat facing the throne
where the ceiling rains poetry
words creep out of the books
and poems jump everywhere

She was sitting with all her dignity
with elegance dripping from her shining eyes
and wisdom pouring from her lips

With a smile spanning the width of her cheeks
she said: I prepared Arabic coffee for you
then, handed the cup over to me
along with some Scottish scones

She gazed out of the window and sighed:
Oh Arthur's Seat,
my soul mate for years
the intimate friend of my loneliness
the keeper of my secret monologue

On the door, she hugged me
whispering: keep poems alive
keep poetry up

I wish, I could go there again
and engrave these words on the window ledge
"My dear poet;
As much as you think of the poem

I think of you
As much as you love poetry
I love you"
And just forget about the Arabic coffee,
the Scottish scones
and Arthur's Seat.

Every Trip I Have Taken to the Royal in Eight Years

Edinburgh Royal Infirmary

Aiko Greig

When German Anne chipped a bone off her hand in our game against Saints, we waited hours at A&E until 3am to be seen. She got an X-ray. They said she'd be fine; gave paracetamol. She drove us home but did not cry. The next day her hand was so swollen she couldn't bend a finger.

★

When I rolled my ankle in the last game of our undefeated champion season, I iced it until we got our medals, my foot still laced in the boot. You carried me on your back to the waiting room. An X-ray. A sprain. Paracetamol. It was sore for weeks and is still bigger than the right one.

★

After a job interview at the stem cell centre, I went for lunch in the cafe on my way back to work, but left with nothing.

★

For 8 months straight, I came every fortnight, then every week, and fin ally every day. I queued with people like me, who wanted to create life. We sat in a room filled with magazines of pregnant celebrities, each of us eyeing only her own empty hands. Sometimes I gave blood. Sometimes a person ran a wand inside my body in a dark room and we counted the ghosts of cysts on TV. Sometimes, after so much measuring, the eggs were the right size. I'd get a jab in my belly to free them and be encouraged to have a 'nice' weekend.

*

We returned for our first scan. I waited for you to arrive and before then, walked in on two separate pregnant women in toilets without the locks latched. I did star jumps in the hallway to make the thing inside me move.

re-use me

Portobello beach

Anne Laure Coxam

where is the metaphor?
because in all the rubbish
you picked the words
re-use me

and I wrote re-use me
on Portobello beach
with the rubbish
abandoned stuff
we collected there

a Tetley tea bag
for the loop of the r
seashells seaweed
razor clams sticks
colourful stones
I still have the picture

it was for an art project
you were doing with
a science fiction writer
and it never worked out

it was difficult
to write words
with rubbish
on the beach

you said it was not
that complicated
but it was windy
and we could barely open
our eyes

so where is the metaphor?
you know
without underwater currents
waves just move in loops
the water is moving but is still
so a bottle
would not drift

you liked my re-use me
you said
I was good at it
– writing words
with rubbish

HRH

Palace of Holyroodhouse

Harry Josephine Giles

I blew you up, fuckers,
sixteen hundred and seventy eight
times with my dire mind,
and once with the hands
of kids we tore you

up. Get out. Such cardboard
won't keep you holy, only
my ribs will, now binding
burnt grief for the awful
loss of something to hate.

NEMO ME IMPUNE LACESSIT

Meadowbank Changing Manifesto

Meadowbank

Colin Herd

We need another word
for badminton. If everyone's
comfortable calling squash
squash, at least for the meantime,
we should consider the following
suggestions: swish, jumpwhack,
trainersqueek shimmyracket,
weirdsport, hurrystyles, nothockey,
ritzyexuberance, breathybeats,
SmashThePants, thintennis,
whichsideamimeanttobeongame,
whatsthescorenowsport,
high-and-fluttery, middlerackety,
deftness, highnet, shuttlecockhitting,
over-the-top, sullyknee, pinstrip,
or how about we play it really
cautious and classy and just
trim the word to *BAD*? We'll take
a vote so it should be pretty
painless. Starting localised
in this sweaty, noise-art
cardboard changing room,
but branching out like a
brakeless shuttlecock that's
been watching Forrest Gump,
we're going to refashion
every sport until the world's
a different and/or better place!

Crags

Salisbury Crags

Iain Matheson

dragons will arrive they will
feast on scrambled eggs they will
study trigonometry

crazed dogs will interrogate
the entrails of plastic bags
they will dig for kryptonite

exact men in drab coats they
will smell of garlic they will
create homes for homeless bugs

On Arthur's Seat

Arthur's Seat

Theresa Muñoz

How do I lean into nothing

walk to the cliff edge
and look over without

falling, like on train platforms
how black those ground wires

and how near to the yellow line
should people loiter

what's the rule now
for getting close to danger,

things in tight passing – cars, buses,
strangers – how safe are we

in rooms of early light
with others we get to know slowly

and how much of our pasts
is too hard to explain

or too tricky, what would happen
if I strode along stamped grass

peered over the edge
into emptiness

trusting myself to the town's tiny lights.

The Royal Yacht Britannia

The Royal Yacht Britannia

Lady Red Ego

You are set in time. Blue
moves, but stillness needs
transparency. Amber royalty.
Every location has already
been reached. Your destination
is your departing.

And what of all these flies
inside your body?
You are the old lady,
you are always eating.
Do we see ourselves as meat?
Or as passing? For we
make you a sewage system,
we go through, we recycle
the time-bit, exist in the limit;
we make you our poem.

A visitor becomes a word,
sentence, stanza, brick-like builds
identity. You cram them in
but they say the same thing,
each synonym repeating.
A Monet impression
is made of spaces;
the water is waving,
you are not sailing.

The Queen of Portobello

Portobello

Hannah McCooke

I moved to Edinburgh with one suitcase
full of short skirts and no winter coat
now I move sofas and dressers,
bag after bag of warm clothes.

Last to come is the cat,
out of the city for the first time.
There is a garden here
windows which open
Coconuts stuffed with birdseed
swing from the washing lines.

No more the breeders pen
the basement of a hotel
one room in a student flat.
No more passed round
this friend or that
everytime the landlord calls.

At sunset the pink light stratifies,
swooping chip fat gulls glow rose.
She watches smokers outside
the Foresters and St Clair's Tattoo.
Bus after bus of day trippers,
sandy dogs in the back of cars.

She never tries to cross the street:
only chews the neighbours plants,
mews from one end of the balcony
to the other.

She can't see the sea from here
but she listens to it.
It is enough to hear the salt cat purr
She is safe. She is satisfied.

Acknowledgements

Our huge thanks go to Noel Chidwick of Shoreline of Infinity, who saw the potential in this project and worked tirelessly to restore it to print. Thank you also to all of the poets and prose writers who contributed their work to Umbrellas of Edinburgh – you were all brilliant, and a pleasure to work with. Thank you to Alan Gillis for his thoughtful and thought provoking introduction, for which we are deeply indebted. Our tremendous thanks and admiration go to Nick Askew, our illustrator, whose artwork adds new depths to this anthology. To the LitLong team, namely Victoria Anker, Tara Thomson and James Loxley, thank you for your advice and financial support without which this collection may never have been born. Huge thankyous to Richard Ridgwell for his proof readings expertise. Thanks also go to Pagemaster Andrew Chidwick. Personal thanks to our friends and family, who are too numerous to mention in totality and whose support, as always, is vital and appreciated. And thank you to all those we haven't named, who had some part in helping to shape and produce this book. We, and Edinburgh, thank you all.

About the Editors

Russell Jones is an Edinburgh-based writer and editor. He has published 6 poetry collections and 1 novel, and edited 3 poetry anthologies. He was the UK's first Pet Poet Laureate and has a PhD in Creative Writing from the University of Edinburgh.

Claire Askew is the author of the poetry collection This changes things (Bloodaxe, 2016); and the novels All The Hidden Truths (2018), What You Pay For (2019) and Cover Your Tracks (2020), published by Hodder & Stoughton. Claire was the 2017 Jessie Kesson Fellow, and has worked as Writer in Residence at the University of Edinburgh and Schools Writer in Residence for both Scottish Book Trust and the Edinburgh International Book Festival. Follow her @ onenightstanzas.

About the Writers

Patricia Ace is the author of the poetry collections First Blood, Fabulous Beast and In Defiance of Short Days. A new collection, The Lido at Night, is forthcoming from Red Squirrel Press. Her work, which explores family, nature, spirituality and the female experience, has been widely anthologised and has found success in many prominent poetry competitions. She lives in rural, central Scotland and works as a yoga teacher and therapist.

Viccy Adams has been a writer in residence with the Naxi people in rural South West China, created a virtual library of books by women, had writing about sewing machines exhibited at the V&A, and burnt a day's work to fuel a mobile sauna. Find her on Twitter/Instagram/Facebook @ViccyIsWriting or www.viccyadams.com

Esa Aldegheri is a Scottish-Italian writer and academic. She is completing a multilingual PhD on forced migration, integration and story exchange. Her writing has been published by Granta, Gutter, The Dangerous Women Project and others. She lives in Edinburgh and is a compulsive climber of trees and reader of maps.

Jane Alexander is the author of two novels, A User's Guide to Make-Believe (2020) and The Last Treasure Hunt (2015). Her short stories have won awards and been widely published. Originally from Aberdeen, Jane has lived in Edinburgh for 20 years, where she teaches creative writing at the University of Edinburgh.

Janette Ayachi is a Scottish-Algerian poet living in Edinburgh. She is the author of two poetry pamphlets and one full collection (Hand Over Mouth Music, Pavillion LUP,

2019) which won a Saltire Literary Award in 2019. She is working on a new book of non-fiction about travelling alone, Lonerlust, and performs her poetry across the U.K.

Ruth Aylett lives in Edinburgh where she teaches and researches university-level computing. Joint author of the pamphlet Handfast, published in 2016, she has been published by The North, Prole, Antiphon, The Lake, New Writing Scotland, South Bank Poetry, Envoi, Bloodaxe Books, Red Squirrel Press, and others. Her pamphlet Pretty in Pink is due out in 2021 with 4Word. See www.macs.hw.ac.uk/~ruth/writing.html for more.

Aileen Ballantyne is a national newspaper journalist turned poet. Her investigative journalism has been commended twice in the British Press Awards. Poetry awards include the prestigious Mslexia Poetry Prize (winner, 2015) and a Scottish Book Trust New Writers Award (2018). Her first collection, Taking Flight (Luath Press, Autumn 2019), includes a series of poems on the Lockerbie disaster. Twitter: @ailyballantyne

Anne Ballard lives in North Edinburgh. Her poems have appeared in Acumen, Orbis, Magma, The Interpreter's House, Poetry Scotland and elsewhere, including the FWS 2018 anthology Spindrift. She won first prize in the Poetry on the Lake Competition 2018. Her pamphlet Family Division was published by in 2015.

Jonathan Bay is a Californian transman who spent several years living, working and studying in Edinburgh. A traveller and former farmhand; he has most been published in Gutter and was a winner of the Jupiter Artland Inspired to Write competition. Jonathan has a PhD in Creative Writing from The University of Edinburgh.

Tessa Berring's poetry collection Bitten Hair was published in 2019 in Edinburgh with Blue Diode Press. She is currently engaged in research around ideas of the 'idiolect' - language for a community of one.

Stella Hervey Birrell is an award-winning poet and author who lives in Midlothian. Her work has been published by the Selkie, the Scottish Book Trust, and more unusually, Scotrail.

Andrew Blair is a writer, poet and performer who co-produces Poetry Shows and podcasts with Ross McCleary, including a spoken-word murder mystery night set in a Ferrero Rocher advert. His pamphlet The R-Pattz Facttz 2020 was published in August by Speculative Books.

Helen Boden was born in Yorkshire, and writes, teaches and edits from the edge of Edinburgh. Widely published in magazines and anthologies including Gutter, New Writing Scotland, Northwords Now, Ink, Sweat and Tears, Antiphon, Mslexia, Lighthouse and Butcher's Dog, she also collaborates with visual artists to make responsive poems and place-specific text. helenbodenliteraryarts.wordpress.com @bodHelen

Marianne Boruch has published 10 poetry collections including her most recent, The Anti-Grief (Copper Canyon, 2019). She has published 3 essay collections about poetry and was the 2012 Fulbright Professor and Fellow at the Institute for Advanced Studies in the Humanities at the University of Edinburgh. She is emeritus from Purdue University, recently returning from Australia and a second Fulbright where she closely observed that country's astonishing wildlife. Her subsequent poetry collection, BESTIARY DARK, is forthcoming from Copper Canyon.

Douglas Bruton has been widely published including in Northwords Now and New Writing Scotland. His stories have won competitions with Fish, HISSAC, Federation of Writers (Scotland), The Neil Gunn Prize and The William Soutar Prize. His novel, Mrs Winchester's Gun Club, was published in 2019 by Scotland Street Press. (douglasrdbruton@hotmail.com)

Kevin Cadwallender lives on Easter Road in Edinburgh. Forty years, many collections, many pamphlets – his poems have featured in many magazines and anthologies. Kevin hates writing biographies almost as much as he hates filling in tax forms. He has written too many books to list here, so he suggests you Google him!

AJ Clay writes LGBTQ+ YA fiction and creative nonfiction, and is a 2016 UNESCO Emerging Writer and Penguin WriteNow 2018 shortlisted author. Their recent work has been published with Monstrous Regiment, Ellipsis Zine, and Scottish Book Trust. @uisgebeatha

Dave Coates gained a PhD at the University of Edinburgh, writing a thesis on Louis MacNeice's influence on Northern Irish poetry. He also runs a poetry blog at davepoems.wordpress.com, which won the 2015 Saboteur Award for Best Reviewer.

Anne Connolly is a widely published Irish poet, long settled in Edinburgh. She has performed at Stanza 2019 and in several Festivals in Ireland. She chaired the Federation of Writers, Scotland 2016 -2018 and was their 2014 Makar. Once upon a Quark(2019) is her third collection from Red Squirrel Press.

Sophie Cooke writes and co-produces film-poems, previously for public events such as the Commonwealth Games' cultural programme and the Year of Natural Scotland. She writes poems in collaboration with composers for musical performance (Remembered/Imagined at Summerhall), and also as site-specific pieces (for the Fruitmarket Gallery). She has won the Genomics Forum Poetry Prize. Also a novelist and short story writer, Sophie Cooke lives with her partner in

Edinburgh where she teaches at Skriva Writing School. www.sophiecooke.com

Anne Laure Coxam has had work published in Local Tongue, LIT, Valve, Zarf, DATABLEED and Poetry Scotland. Her first pamphlet, Toolbox Therapy, was published by Sad Press in 2016.

Tim Craven has an MFA from Syracuse University and is completing his PhD at the University of Edinburgh. His pamphlet, Lake Effect, is published by Tapsalteerie, and he was the 2018/19 Writer-in-Residence at the Isle of Harris Distillery. www.timcraven.co.uk

Christine De Luca writes in English and Shetlandic. She was Edinburgh's Makar for 2014-2017. Besides children's stories and one novel, she has had seven poetry collections and four bi-lingual volumes published. She's participated in many festivals here and abroad. Her poems have been selected four times for the Best Scottish Poems of the Year.

Keith Dumble is an author from Edinburgh. Winner of several short story awards, he has also appeared at the Edinburgh International Book Festival's Story Shop. Inspired by folklore, mythology and the metaphysical, he is currently writing a novel exploring themes of mortality and grief via the concept of reincarnation.

Sally Evans is a widely published poet whose recent books include Bewick Walks to Scotland (2006), The Bees (2008), The Honey Seller (2009), Poetic Adventures in Scotland (2014), The Grecian Urn (2015) and Anderson's Piano (2016). She has edited 91 issues of Poetry Scotland. She is Poetry Editor of the Scots Language Centre website and edits Keep Poems Alive.

Bashabi Fraser is a poet, children's writer, translator, critic, editor and academic. She has been widely published and anthologised. Her recent publications include Letters to my Mother and Other Mothers (2015), Ragas & Reels (2012), Scots Beneath the Banyan Tree: Stories from Bengal (2012); From the Ganga to the Tay (an epic poem, 2009). Her awards include the 2015 Outstanding Woman of Scotland (Saltire Society), Women Empowered: Arts and Culture Award and the AIO Prize for Literary Services in Scotland.

Miriam Gamble is from Belfast, but now lives in Edinburgh. Her collections are The Squirrels Are Dead (2010), which won a Somerset Maugham Award in 2011, Pirate Music (2014) and What Planet (2019), all published by Bloodaxe.

Harry Josephine Giles is from Orkney and lives in Leith. Their latest book is The Games (Out-Spoken Press), shortlisted for the 2019 Saltire Prize for Best Collection. They have a PhD in Creative Writing from Stirling, co-direct the performance platform Anatomy, and are touring the poetry-music-video show Drone internationally. www. harryjosephine.com

Marjorie Lotfi Gill's poems have been widely published in journals and anthologies, including Acumen, Ambit, Gutter, Magma, Mslexia, The North, Rattle, The Reader and The Rialto, and have been performed on BBC Radio 4. She was the Poet in Residence at Jupiter Artland (2014-2016) and the Writer in Residence for both Spring Fling and the 2015 Wigtown Book Festival. She is also a co-founder of The Belonging Project, a series of workshops reflecting on the flight, journey and assimilation of refugees.

Jane Goldman is Reader in English Literature at Glasgow University and likes anything a word can do. Her poems have been published in Adjacent Pineapple, Gutter, Scree, Stand, Tender, Zarf, and elsewhere. Her first slim volume is Border Thoughts (Leamington Books, 2014), and her new collection

SEKXPHRASTICS is forthcoming with Dostoyevsky Wannabe

Pippa Goldschmidt is the author of the novel The Falling Sky and the short story collection The Need for Better Regulation of Outer Space. Her recent work has been broadcast on Radio 4, and published in Mslexia, Litro, A Year of Scottish Poems and Multiverse. She's also co-editor of Uncanny Bodies (Luna Press), an anthology of creative and academic work inspired by Freud's uncanny. Tune in to @goldipipschmidt.

Stephanie Green's most recent pamphlet is Flout (HappenStance, 2015). Her poetry was set to music by Marisa Sharon Hartanto at the St Magnus Festival, 2013, and inspired a dance choreographed by Mathew Hawkins, Edinburgh, 2015. Berlin Umbrella, a collaboration with Sound Artist, Sonja Heyer, launched in Berlin, 2018. She is also a theatre and dance reviewer. www.stephaniegreen.org.uk

Aiko Greig was born in California and now lives in Scotland where she completed an MSc in Creative Writing at the University of Edinburgh. Aiko won a Scottish Book Trust New Writers Award in 2015. Her poetry is published in The Edinburgh Review, Dactyl, and Ink Sweat & Tears, among others. www.lionandsloth.com

Jane Griffiths is a former lecturer at the University of Edinburgh, and is now Associate Professor at Oxford and Tutorial Fellow of Wadham College. The most recent of her five Bloodaxe poetry collections, Silent in Finisterre (2017), was a Poetry Book Society Recommendation. Her (largely non-verbal) website is https://poetandcat.design

Dominic Hale helps put together the poetry zines CUMULUS and MOTE, and co-organises the reading series JUST NOT.

Anne Hay has published poems in Envoi, Gutter, Magma, Interpreter's House and Northwords Now. She won a Scottish Book Trust New Writer's Award in 2020. annehaypoetry.com.

Iyad Hayatleh is a Palestinian poet and translator. Born and brought up in a Palestinian refugee camp in Syria, Iyad has lived in Glasgow since 2000, giving many readings and workshops around the country. His first collection, Beyond all Measure, was published by Survivor's Press in 2007. Iyad has collaborated with the poet Tessa Ransford on a two-way translation project resulting in the book Rug of a Thousand Colours (Luath, 2012), inspired by the Five Pillars of Islam. He has also collaborated with Palestinian artist Manl Deeb: they published an eBook, Homeland (Palestinian visual art and poetry from diaspora)

Andy Jackson recently published his third poetry collection The Saints Are Coming via Blue Diode (2020). He has also edited several anthologies including Split Screen, Double Bill, Whaleback City (with W.N.Herbert) and Scotia Extremis (with Brian Johnstone). www.andyjacksonpoet.co.uk

Snigdha Koirala is a poet and writer based in New York City. Her works have appeared in Glass: A Journal of Poetry, Wildness, Gutter, and elsewhere. She is a graduate student at NYU's Centre for Experimental Humanities, where, amongst other things, she explores the sedimentation of violence and history in the English language.

Lady Red Ego is a lesbian writer who has previously been published in anthologies such as We Were Always Here by Queer Words Project Scotland, Crossing Lines by Broken Sleep Books, Multiverse by Shorelines of Infinity, and Dark Animals by Wild Pressed Books. Her first pamphlet, The Red Ego, was published by Wild Pressed Books in 2019, and her second Pamphlet, Natural Sugars, was published by Broken Sleep Books in August this year.

Dorothy Lawrenson is a Dundee-born poet, educated in Texas and Edinburgh, where she now lives. Her poems have appeared in Gutter, Edinburgh Review, Irish Pages and Lallans, and in the anthologies A Year of Scottish Poems, Best Scottish Poetry, Be the First to Like This, Double Bill, and Whaleback City. www.dorothylawrenson.com

Màrtainn Mac an t-Saoir / Martin MacIntyre is originally from Lenzie, Glasgow. He is an author, poet and storyteller. His novels and short stories have been nominated for several prizes,and he has won the Saltire First Book Award. Martin's poetry has been published in Dannsam Led Fhaileas / Let Me Dance With Your Shadow. In 2007, he was crowned 'Bàrd' by An Comunn Gàidhealach and he has been a member of Shore Poets since 2010.

Peter Mackay has published two collections of poems with Acair: Gu Leòr / Galore and Nàdur De / Some Kind of. Originally from the Isle of Lewis, he is a lecturer in Literature at the University of St Andrews and lives in Edinburgh.

Rob A. Mackenzie lives in Leith. He is reviews editor for Magma Poetry magazine and co-organises monthly Edinburgh live poetry event, Vespers. He runs literary publishing house, Blue Diode Press. His third full collection, The Book of Revelation, was published by Salt in 2020.

Aonghas MacNeacail, poet and songwriter, was born in Uig, on the Isle of Skye. He is also a broadcaster, journalist, scriptwriter, librettist and translator. A native Gael, he writes in Gaelic and English.

Marianne MacRae is an Edinburgh-based poet. Her work has appeared in Ambit, Acumen, Magma and Gutter and she was the 2017/18 poet-in-residence at The Royal College of Physicians and Surgeons of Glasgow. Her pamphlet, Recital, is forthcoming from Tapsalteerie.

Agnes Marton is a poet, writer, Reviews Editor of The Ofi Press, Fellow of the Royal Society of Arts. Recent publications include her collection Captain Fly's Bucket List, the award-winning Estuary: A Confluence of Art and Poetry and four chapbooks with Moria Books. She won the National Poetry Day Competition.

Iain Matheson was born in Plean and grew up in Glasgow. He now lives is Edinburgh where he is a long-time composer and recent poet. His poetry has been published by House of Three Press, in Gutter magazine, and in Spark (published by Blue Diode Press).

Richie McCaffery lives in Ghent, Belgium and holds a PhD in Scottish Literature from the University of Glasgow. His has published two pamphlets of poetry as well as a book-length collection (Cairn from Nine Arches Press). He has another pamphlet forthcoming in 2017 and is nearly finished a collection of poems based on his new life in Belgium.

Hannah McCooke has been published in Dear Damsels, The Selkie, and Blood Bath Literary Zine. Her debut pamphlet 'Mortal Magic' was released in 2019. Originally from Northern Ireland, her work is preoccupied with cliff-edges, eggs, seaweed and lesbians.

Colin McGuire's most recent poetry collection was 'Enhanced Fool Disclosure' published by Speculative Books. He won the 'Out:Spoken Award in 2018 in London for best film poem and best poem and was also a Scottish Book Trust Ignite Awardee in 2020. www.colinmcguirepoet.co.uk

Jane McKie has several poetry publications, some resulting from collaborations with artists. Morocco Rococo won the Sundial/SAC award for best first book of 2007. Her most recent collection is Quiet Woman, Stay (Cinnamon Press). She is currently a Senior Lecturer in Creative Writing at the

University of Edinburgh, and is a member of Edinburgh-based Shore Poets as well as the 12 collective of women writers.

nick-e melville has thirteen publications. His last was ABBODIES (Sad Press, 2017) - about Aliens, Brexit, Bodies and ABBA - and he is currently completing the sequel ABBODIES COLD.

Ricky Monahan Brown is author of the memoir Stroke, a Scotsman Scottish Book of 2019. He won the FWS 20for2020 microflash competition and was shortlisted for the Friday Flash Fiction Edinburgh Festival Award. Ricky Is completing a short story collection and a film script set in the nineteenth century Highlands.

Iain Morrison's collection I'm a Pretty Circler was published by Vagabond Voices in 2018 and nominated for the Saltire Prize. His work is included in the book Makar/Unmakar: Twelve Contemporary Poets in Scotland (Tapsalteerie, 2019).

Theresa Muñoz lives in Edinburgh. She is a Research Associate at Newcastle University and organises the Newcastle Poetry Festival. Her work has recently appeared in Poetry Review, Wild Court, Canadian Literature, and A Year of Scottish Poems. Her debut collectio Settle shortlisted for the Melita Hume Poetry Prize. In 2018 she won a Creative Scotland Muriel Spark Centenary Award and a Robert Louis Stevenson Fellowship

Louise Peterkin is a poet from Edinburgh. In 2016 She was the recipient of a New Writers Award from the Scottish Book Trust in the Poetry category. Her first poetry collection The Night Jar will be published by Salt in 2020.

Alycia Pirmohamed is the author of two chapbooks, Faces that Fled the Wind (BOAAT Press) and Hinge (ignitionpress). She is the winner of the 2020 Edwin Morgan Poetry Award, and the co-founder and co-director of the Scottish BAME Writers Network. Find her online at @a_pirmohamed.

Rachel Plummer lives in Edinburgh, where they write poems and knit Christmas stockings. Their latest book, Wain, is a collection of LGBT poems for young readers. Rachel is a Scottish Book Trust New Writers Award recipient, has two children, three guinea pigs, and entirely too many books.

Lauren Pope's poetry pamphlet, Announce This (Templar Poetry), was shortlisted for the Callum Macdonald Memorial Awards. Her poetry has appeared in various publications including Gutter, Magma, The North, Poetry Wales, The Rialto and Best New British and Irish Poets 2017 (Eyewear Publishing). She is a Manchester Poetry Prize finalist.

Chris Powici's most recent collection is This Weight of Light, published by Red Squirrel. A new book of his poems is due in 2021. Chris Lives in Perthshire. He teaches creative writing for The Open University and The University of Stirling.

Elizabeth Rimmer has published three poetry collections with Red Squirrel Press, Wherever We Live Now (2011), The Territory of Rain (2015) and Haggards (2018). She writes about nature, wild landscapes, ways of knowing and about social upheaval and regeneration. She also edits new poets for Red Squirrel Press. www.burnedthumb.co.uk.

Tracey S. Rosenberg is Writer in Residence at Edinburgh University, and the author of the historical novel The Girl in the Bunker and the poetry collection Secondary. She likes cats, and Evensong, and very long train rides. She has a tattoo from Easter Island.

Finola Scott's poems are widely published including in The Fenland Reed, New Writing Scotland, Gutter, and The Ofi Press. Red Squirrel will publish her pamphlet in October.

Tapsalteerie will publishing her Scots poems in the New Year. A winner of various competitions, she is on Facebook at Finola Scott Poems.

Sophie Scrivener (b. 1994) is from Northamptonshire, England, currently living in Tartu, Estonia. She is a full-time translation editor and all-other-times writer. Her poems have been published in anthologies by Beautiful Dragons Press.

Emma Sedlak is a Scottish-American writer-singer-poet (which means she would have been great as a minstrel or scribe a few hundred years ago!). She currently lives in Sydney, Australia with her partner and son, where she works at the University of New South Wales. You can find Emma at EmmaSedlak.com, or on Twitter as @thebedsidepoet

Roddy Shippin is from Edinburgh. He co-ran Blind Poetics and Poets Against Humanity. Poems of his have also appeared in places like Gutter, Magma and Aiblins: New Scottish Political Poetry. His first pamphlet - Curriculum Vitae - was published by the QuemPress and was second place in the 2018 Calum Macdonald Award.

Nancy Somerville's work has been widely published in anthologies and magazines. She writes mainly poetry but has finished the first draft of a novel. Her short story Mountain Avens won the Scottish Mountain Writing competition in 2015. Her poetry collection, Waiting for Zebras was published by Red Squirrel Press (Scotland) in 2008. www.redsquirrelpress.com. In 2004 she co-edited with Stewart Conn, Goldfish Suppers, an illustrated poetry anthology for families with young children.

Jock Stein is a piper and preacher from East Lothian. He brings to his poetry experience of the Sheffield steel industry, life in East Africa, directing a conference centre, a sabbatical in Hungary, and the politics of Scotland today. He writes poetry in many styles, serious and quirky. Google Handsel Press Sanctus Media Store.

Gerda Stevenson, award-winning writer/actor/director/ singer-songwriter; her stage and radio plays, short stories, opera libretto, and poetry widely performed, broadcast and published, including Federer versus Murray (Salmagundi, USA), If This Were Real (Smokestack Books) published in Italian translation Se Questo Fosse Vero (Edizioni Ensemble); Quines: Poems in tribute to women of Scotland, (Luath Press). www.gerdastevenson.co.uk

Sarah Stewart's poetry can be found in Ambit, Magma, The Keats-Shelley Review, Best Scottish Poems and more. Her first pamphlet, Glisk (Tapsalteerie) won the 2019 Callum Macdonald Memorial Award. She writes children's fiction under the pseudonym Sarah Forbes.

Alice Tarbuck is a poet living in Edinburgh. Her first pamphlet, Grid, was published by Sad Press in spring 2018. Her work has been commissioned by Durham Literary Festival, the Sheffield Post Office Gallery, the University of Edinburgh, Scottish PEN, and Timespan in Helmsdale. She is part of 12, an Edinburgh women's poetry collective and is a 2019 Scottish Book Trust New Writers Awardee.

Sandy Thomson likes stories because you don't pay for special effects. She's made theatre and film across the world. She's a Playwright Studio Scotland Award winner and her recent projects include Damned Rebel Bitches - a geriatric action/adventure and American Dream a short film about time travel and self murder.

Samuel Tongue's first collection is Sacrifice Zones (Red Squirrel. 2020). He also has two pamphlets, Stitch (Tapsalteerie, 2018) and Hauling Out (Eyewear, 2016).

Samuel works as Project Coordinator at the Scottish Poetry Library. @SamuelTongue

Hamish Whyte is an Edinburgh-based poet, editor and publisher. He runs Mariscat Press, which in 2015 won both the Callum Macdonald Memorial Award and the Michael Marks Award for poetry pamphlet publishing. He was an RLS Fellow in 2007 and is an Honorary Research Fellow in Scottish Literature, University of Glasgow. His third collection from Shoestring Press, Things We Never Knew, is published in 2016. He is a member of Edinburgh's Shore Poets and plays percussion in the band The Whole Shebang.

Colin Will is an Edinburgh-born writer, editor and saxophonist. He has had eleven books published, the latest being Word Play (short stories), published by Postbox Press in 2018. Website: www.colinwill.co.uk

JL Williams' books include Condition of Fire, Locust and Marlin, House of the Tragic Poet and After Economy. She is interested in expanding dialogues through writing across languages, perspectives and cultures and in multimodal and cross-form work, visual art, dance, opera and theatre. @jlwpoetry www.jlwilliamspoetry.co.uk

Andrew J. Wilson lives in Edinburgh. His work has appeared in Multiverse: An International Anthology of Science Fiction Poetry, Scotia Extremis: Poems from the Extremes of Scotland's Psyche, Eye to the Telescope and many other places. With Neil Williamson, he co-edited the award-nominated anthology Nova Scotia: New Scottish Speculative Fiction.

Ryan Van Winkle lives in Edinburgh. His second collection, The Good Dark, won the Saltire Society's 2015 Poetry Book of the Year award. His poems have appeared in New Writing Scotland, The Prairie Schooner, The American

Poetry Review, AGNI and Best Scottish Poems 2015. He was awarded a Robert Louis Stevenson fellowship in 2012 and a residency at The Studios of Key West in 2016. As a member of Highlight Arts he has organized festivals and workshops in Syria, Pakistan and Iraq.

Jay GYing is a Chinese-Scottish writer, critic and translator from Edinburgh. Currently he is an MFA candidate at Brown University. He is the author of two pamphlets: Wedding Beasts (2019) and Katabasis (2020). He is a Contributing Editor at The White Review and Assistant Poetry Editor at Asymptote.

JaneYolen is within 9 books of having 400 books published, and has won a great many awards for her books and writing. One of those awards set her good coat on fire.

Nick Askew is an illustrator and artist living and working in Edinburgh.You can find more of his work on instagram @alittlebitaskew

Index